CORRESPONDENCE WITH A CRIPPLE FROM TARSUS

Also by H. Beecher Hicks, Jr. . . .
Preaching Through a Storm

CORRESPONDENCE WITH A CRIPPLE FROM TARSUS

Romans In Dialogue With The 20TH Century

H. BEECHER HICKS JR.

Foreword by Wyatt Tee Walker

Ministry Resources Library

Zondervan Publishing House • Grand Rapids, MI

Ministry Resources Library is an imprint of Zondervan Publishing House,
1415 Lake Drive, S.E., Grand Rapids, Michigan 49506.

All Scripture quotations, unless otherwise noted, are taken from the King James
Version of the Bible.

Edited by Joseph Comanda

Printed in the United States of America

Library of Congress Cataloging in Publication Data

Hicks, H. Beecher
    Correspondence with a cripple from Tarsus : Romans in dialogue with the
twentieth century / H. Beecher Hicks, Jr. ; foreword by Wyatt Tee Walker.
      p.   cm.
    ISBN 0-310-52201-3
    1. Bible. N.T. Romans—Sermons. 2. Bible. N.T. Romans—Miscellanea.
3. Imaginary letters. 4. Baptists—Sermons. 5. Sermons, American—Afro-
American authors. I. Title.
BS2665.4.H53   1990   90-35564
252'.061—dc20   CIP

90 · 91 92 93 94 95 / AF / 10 9 8 7 6 5 4 3 2 1

Dear Daddy:

You have been the inspiration for my preaching, my ministry, and my life. There is nothing that I have ever done or will ever do that I did not learn by your precept and example. Any seas I have conquered, any storms I have endured are due in large measure to the charted course you set and the mercy of the Pilot about whom you have constantly preached. Seminaries can never teach on purpose the lessons you have shared by accident. For all you do, this book's for you.

Love,
Henry, Jr.

CONTENTS

FOREWORD

Correspondence with a Cripple from Tarsus is a fantasy with substance. Beecher Hicks has fine-tuned his literary and preaching gifts with this innovative exchange of letters between a sensitive urban pastor and the greatest letter writer of all time, the apostle Paul. As much as anything else, the reader is jarred into the reality that Paul's letters were never intended to be "books" of a Bible; they were correspondence with Christians of the early church struggling to appropriate the gospel of Jesus Christ into their daily lives.

If you are not familiar with the message of Paul's letter to the church at Rome, this volume will send you scurrying to read it. It is the singular most important book of the New Testament literature. Dr. Hicks unfolds its substance and meaning with careful detail that is neither cumbersome nor wearying. He has struck a marvelous balance of narrative and sermon. The "correspondence" prevents the sermons from being pedantic, and the narrative provides sufficient historical context for the full meaning of the sermons to be grasped.

This book is almost a time machine in print. With it the author helps us to look into the world of Paul, even as Paul tries to look into our world of today. By juxtaposing those two worlds, Hicks leads us into a deeper appreciation of how Paul's message came out of the early church's struggle to grow.

Correspondence with a Cripple from Tarsus is an important book for all earnest Christians, lay and clergy. It will be especially useful to clergy. It has the twin values of "checking" Hicks' assumptions and conclusions against the record of

Romans and, at the same time, of feeding our own preaching as he wrestles with some of the great tenets of Christian faith.

The author has succeeded in retaining the flavor of traditional African-American preaching while using the medium of writing. It is not an easy task to fit that which comes out of an oral tradition into a literary form. Beecher has done justice to both.

Read this book and reap generous spiritual benefit. It embraces the essence of the pristine faith of the early church in the field preacher from Galilee. It embraces that marvelous and complex personality, the apostle Paul of Tarsus. Read this book! It will help you to become a better disciple of the Lord Jesus Christ.

Wyatt Tee Walker
Canaan Baptist Church of Christ
Harlem, New York

PREFACE

All too often Sunday morning sermons bore us. That being the case, it's not so likely that we'd choose to read them during the week. As a consequence, for the average person to read one sermon is a rarity; to read an entire book of them may well be an act of charity, if not an act of grace. Yet now that you have opened this book, I trust that you will see it through to the end. While it is a book of sermons, it is also something more than that.

Over the past twelve months I have been engaged in a great odyssey, a great adventure of both preaching and teaching within the loving, eclectic, and electric preaching setting of the Metropolitan pulpit, which I am blessed to serve. We have set our course, Metropolitan and I, on a venture of faith through the epistle of Paul to the Romans. Week in and week out we have sought to engage both mind and spirit in an examination of the theology and thought of the Apostle from Tarsus. This volume will permit the reader to travel with us from point to point in what is perhaps the most pivotal book in the whole of the New Testament.

There are many scholarly books on Paul's writings. This book is not one of them, nor is it intended to be a work of pioneering scholarship, even though we have sought to honor scholarly methodology. What we have here is simply the faithful recording of those moments of interaction between pastor and people, in concert with the direction and leading of the Holy Spirit. As much as possible, I have sought to retain the integrity of the text as it was preached, with only minimal editorial corrections to facilitate the reading process.

God be thanked for the patient people of the Metropolitan Church, who have "endured the toil" of these sermons in the moment of the preaching event. I am grateful to the members of my staff, most especially Mrs. Pamela Ashton for invaluable production assistance and Mrs. Beatrice R. Coker, whose creative prodding encouraged the publication of this volume. In addition, I am appreciative for the counsel and wisdom of my fellow-sufferers in the gospel, the Reverend Albert Gallmon of the Mount Carmel Baptist Church and the Reverend Everett C. Goodwin of the First Baptist Church, both of Washington, D.C.

A WORD ON STRUCTURE

This book is intended, in every sense of the word, to be a correspondence with the apostle Paul. It seems fair. The apostle Paul is responsible for the writing of two-thirds of the New Testament. He did not write books or chapters or verses. He wrote letters. How strange that after all these years—and we must not forget that although he ultimately wrote *for us* he did not write *to us*—no one, it seems, ever bothered to answer his letters with a written reply. If any such replies do exist, they have not been preserved for our generation.

Each chapter except the last has a three-part structure: prologue, sermon, and epilogue. The prologue consists of a letter written to the apostle Paul from this preacher (in a typeface resembling that of a typewriter). Next, the sermon seeks to address the issues raised in the correspondence. The sermon is, in turn, followed by an epilogue, a responsive critique from Paul to the preacher and to you (in a typeface resembling script).

It is my hope that the format of this work will have a twofold advantage.

First, it will permit those who are engaged in the work of ministry to share in the musings and amusings of a fellow-preacher struggling for meaningful dialogue between a first-century writer and contemporary Christians.

While this work is personal, it is also universal in scope. Every preacher who is engaged in a romance with the Word longs to be able to speak firsthand with those about whom he has so often preached.

At the same time, it may well be that the end result of this effort will be a kind of prophetic transparency which permits others to see the preacher/person who thinks and feels and questions and doubts. It will assuredly permit those of us who wear priestly robes to see ourselves in those lights of questioning and doubt which we have hidden from ourselves. At the very least we have here a sharing of thoughts and perceptions about the craft of preaching which many preachers hold privately but almost never reveal publicly.

Second, the layman will benefit as we walk together through the issues which the Scripture raises whether or not they show up in the sermon itself. This work will permit the average church member to understand how the preacher thinks, an inside view of the struggle of thought and spirit which is often not communicated as the word from the pulpit reaches the pew.

One must constantly bear in mind, however, that this is one preacher's perspective, which is not normative for others.

The correspondence between parson and apostle is written from the vantage point of that Saturday-night scramble for a sermon with which too many preachers are painfully familiar, followed by the Monday morning recap for which most preachers have a dread worse than death.

Scholars find hints of the presence of a redactor in Paul's letter to the church at Rome, someone in particular to whom he addresses his rhetorical questions and who bears the brunt of his not infrequent diatribes and flights of argumentation. Perhaps you and I shall be that "someone." Together we shall raise the questions and argue the points until we make sense of Paul or Paul makes sense of us.

Admittedly, putting "words in the mouth" of another—especially someone of Paul's stature—is an audacious act. In doing so, I am not trying to "out-Paul" Paul or to rewrite Scripture. Instead, I have tried to employ what one might call "sanctified imagination" to help us climb into the mind of this limping cripple from Tarsus and absorb his soul into our own.

What we have here is an honest attempt at dialogue, exchange, give-and-take, conversation and correspondence, if you will, between two preachers of two very different generations. Such a correspondence should not seem so far-fetched to us. We live in an era which has a fascination for moving backward and forward in time. If it is possible for us to roll back the curtain of time to see what happened in Paul's *then*, imagination says that Paul may have wanted to "fast-forward" to our *now*. This correspondence, then, takes place at the intersection of *fast-forward* and *reverse* where Paul comes alive in our minds, in our hearts, and in the word we preach.

It must be acknowledged that sermons are never purely original. They are the product of our experience and of lessons taught and principles shared by others along our path. I do not know how many fellow preachers or authors have influenced the frame or the content of the sermons I have preached. If I have infringed upon them in any way, I offer my gratitude as well as my profound apology.

The reader must bear in mind that preaching was never intended to be a monologue. Preaching is most authentically dialogue. Sermons were never meant to be read. They are meant to be heard, experienced, and responded to in the context of a worshiping community, in the context of a preaching moment. Similarly, letters were never intended to be written and lost. Letters were meant to be read and absorbed and internalized and answered. It is exciting to think what we might say to Paul if we had the chance. It is frightening to think what Paul might say to us if he had the same opportunity. One never knows what yesterday might say to today. Share with me this *Correspondence with a Cripple from Tarsus*.

And lest I should be exalted above measure through the abundance of the revelations, there was given to me a thorn in the flesh, the messenger of Satan to buffet me, lest I should be exalted above measure. For this thing I besought the Lord thrice, that it might depart from me. And he said unto me, My grace is sufficient for thee: for my strength is made perfect in weakness. Most gladly therefore will I rather glory in my infirmities, that the power of Christ may rest upon me. Therefore I take pleasure in infirmities, in reproaches, in necessities, in persecutions, in distresses for Christ's sake: for when I am weak, then am I strong (2 Corinthians 12:7–10).

1

CALLED TO BE SAINTS

PROLOGUE

Washington, D.C.
A.D. 1989

Dear Paul:

You don't know me, but I have been an admirer of yours for many years. I've just been reading the letter that you sent to the church at Rome, and I've decided it's about time I wrote to you. Though we are each from a different time and place, I have been assured that you will be able to receive this letter.

I am the pastor of the Metropolitan Church in Washington, and I am living in the twentieth century (almost two thousand years after the birth of Christ). I don't suppose you've ever heard of Washington. It didn't exist in your day, but today it is the capital of a new land across the ocean called the United States of America.

I imagine you're really shocked that we still have copies of your letters around after all this time. We still have them all right, and you would be surprised by the circulation. Your letters have been translated and re-translated (you would not believe how many versions we have), and, Paul, there are churches all over the world that have your name—St. Paul! Who would have thought it? Would you?

But, Paul, you haven't heard it all. Your letters are now used as the basis of many of our sermons in our churches on Sunday morning. Now we know that you meant these letters as very personal notes to some people with whom you had established small churches, but we preachers have taken the liberty to dissect your letters and make up sermons about what you wrote. In fact, we have looked so closely at your writing that we have numbered each sentence for easy reference, and we use them as what we call a <u>text.</u> Sometimes I fear we have taken great freedom (even license) with what you wrote—all this speculating and philosophizing and theologizing about what you meant and intended.

So you understand that is why I needed to write to you now, Paul. I hope you don't mind, but I've been reading and rereading that letter you wrote to the Christian people at Rome. Now that was a letter! You really outdid yourself. But there are some questions that I haven't been able to resolve. After all, you lived in the first century and we live in the twentieth—almost the twenty-first—century, and we're not always sure we've made the proper transition or translation. Sometimes we're not sure what you meant. And sometimes we're not sure that you are sure what you meant. We need your help.

For instance, when you wrote to those new Christian converts in Rome, it appears that they were scared out of their wits. Nero was acting crazy, and folk were being fed to the lions, and they had to live in underground cemeteries. Paul, you wrote these scared people and told them they were "called to be saints." Paul, what's a saint? It's sort of hard to be a saint when lions are chewing at your legs. What's a saint? Did you really think that folk then could be <u>perfect,</u> and is that what you expect for us to be now?

So, Paul, I read what you said about being saints, and I put together a sermon on it. Here's a copy of the sermon, and if you could read it and perhaps jot down a few notes on how it should have been preached, I would appreciate it greatly. Hope the sermon doesn't bore you. I look to hear from you soon.

Sincerely,
Beecher

P.S.: I also hope you won't mind if I share our correspondence with some of my other pastor friends and with some of the Christians in the households where we minister. I am sure that reading this exchange will do us all good.

Sermon: CALLED TO BE SAINTS

Paul, a servant of Jesus Christ, called to be an apostle, separated unto the gospel of God, (Which he had promised afore by his prophets in the holy scriptures,) Concerning his Son Jesus Christ our Lord which was made of the seed of David according to the flesh; And declared to be the Son of God with power, according to the spirit of holiness, by the resurrection from the dead: By whom we have received grace and apostleship, for obedience to the faith among all nations, for his name: Among whom are ye also the called of Jesus Christ: To all that be in Rome, beloved of God, *called to be saints:* Grace to you and peace from God our Father, and the Lord Jesus Christ (Romans 1:1–7).

There is no question in my mind that the book of Romans stands at the core and center of New Testament thought. There can be no controversy or debate that Paul's writings to the church situated at Rome have become, over nearly two centuries of time, the bedrock of Christian doctrine and the starting point for any understanding of Christian theology.

It is clearly true that one who fails to understand the book of Romans will most assuredly fail to understand the whole of the Bible. One writer has suggested that it is as if in this letter Paul were writing his theological last will and testament. Look closely here, for Paul distills into these few pages and sentences the very essence of his faith and belief.

19

Here, in the book of Romans, the great watchwords of our faith are examined and defined.

Here, in the book of Romans, Paul writes with awesome detail of his own understanding of the righteousness of God. Here . . .

Paul stands in the priestly and prophetic tradition to deal
• With Jews and Greeks,
• The wise and the unwise.

Paul deals with such weighty matters as
• Sin and salvation,
• Sanctification and justification.

Paul defines
• What it is to be a church, and
• The importance and priority of preaching within the church.

It is here, in this book, that Paul, the preacher, looks back across the chasm of history and picks a favorite phrase out of Habakkuk's prophetic notebook and then pins the whole of Christianity upon it when he declares:

THE JUST SHALL LIVE BY FAITH!

This is the reason, then, that I wanted to examine Paul's writing to the church at Rome. It is simply because there is no question in my mind that the book of Romans stands at the core and the center of New Testament thought.

The reader of Paul's writing ought to be reminded that what we have here was not intended or designed for common consumption or universal exposure. Paul did not write *to* us even though, of necessity, he did write *for* us.

Paul did not write to the twentieth century. He wrote to the first century.

Paul did not write to a highly organized church or to a sophisticated urban congregation. He wrote to little huddles of persons—outcasts within the enclaves of the Jewish community—who did not worship in grand cathedrals but in churches that started in someone's house.

Paul wrote to those little bands of believers who were struggling to make sense of a Savior who was slaughtered on Calvary and who were trying to live by the principles of a barefoot Galilean whom some say was resurrected on Easter Sunday morning.

Make no mistake about it, Paul did not write to *us*; he wrote to *them*. We simply have the opportunity to look over the shoulder of history, as it were, and read a letter written to a specific people, in a specific time, by a specific preacher.

Paul's letter bore the date stamp of 58 A.D. and the return address of the ancient city of Corinth. Paul's desire was to deliver the letter himself. But before he could go to Spain and get to Rome (for which he had longed and desired) he had to return to Jerusalem with a "love offering" that had been gathered for those who were in need.

Surprisingly, Paul's letter was not delivered by his traveling companions:

- Not by Timothy or Luke.
- Not by Barnabas or John Mark.

Paul's letter was entrusted into the hands of a deaconess, Phoebe by name.

Paul's letter was penned by his own hand:

> To all that be in Rome,
> beloved of God,
> called to be saints,
> Grace to you, and peace
> from God our Father,
> and the Lord Jesus Christ.

Let me confess that I am aware that one does not usually seek to preach from these few rather uninteresting, seemingly casual comments which serve as prologue to Paul's writing. Paul has weightier matters with which to deal in the body of his text. We must be sure, however, that we observe the defined relationship between the writer and the reader and that we note, at the outset, that Paul is about the business of defining who and what he is.

Paul's Definition of Paul

In the first instance, says the writer, I am "Paul, a servant of Jesus Christ."

More precisely, according to the Greek, I am Paul, a *doulos*.

- I am Paul, a slave—one whose will is consumed in Jesus.
- I am Paul, a slave—one who has a permanent relationship of servitude to the Savior.

If you want to know who I am or what I am, I am a servant. . . . I am a slave.

In the second instance, Paul defines himself by saying "not only am I a servant, not only am I a slave, but I am *called to be an apostle.*"

In other words, there is no question, there is no ecclesiastical identity crisis, there is no confusion in my own mind regarding the nature of my calling. And, parenthetically, I must tell you that there is something wrong with a preacher who is not sure of the authenticity of the call.

- Called—a divine summons.
- Called—a divine imperative.
- Called—an anointment as well as an appointment.

Paul says: "I am a servant . . . called to be an apostle!"

In the third instance, Paul says: "I am a servant. Yes, I am called. Yes, I am an apostle. But more than that, I am *separated unto the gospel of God.*"

In other words, he says: *"There is something different about me."*

- There is something strange about this preacher.
- There is something peculiar about this preacher.

I AM SEPARATED!

- I am set apart from the world.
- I am disassociated from the culture.
- I have withdrawn from the wicked.
- I am now distinguished from the demonic.
- I am separated.

My life has new focus; my life has a new direction. My purpose is not about bad news, I am about Good News. I am "separated unto the gospel of God."

Paul takes this moment not only to define who he is but to define who we are and to whom he is writing:

> To all that be in Rome,
> Beloved of God,
> Called to be saints.

Paul's Definition of Us

There is something singularly peculiar in the fact that Paul is writing to the residents of a city to which he has never been. The Roman church is the one church to which Paul writes that he did not found and whose members, with a few exceptions, he had never met. Paul does not know them and knows very little about them. Yet, at the same time he writes "to all that be in Rome." The implication here is clear:

THE GOSPEL SPEAKS TO OUR NEED EVEN IF THE PREACHER
NEGLECTS TO CALL US BY NAME.

Paul did not know who they were individually, but he did know what they were experiencing.

To all that be in Rome:

- You are citizens of the capital of the world. Everyone knows "All roads lead to Rome!"
- You are the citizens of a society ruled by Nero, the son of Agrippina and the adopted child of Claudius.
- You are the unfortunate subjects of a madman named Nero.
  - Nero—a man so depraved that he would put his own wife and mother to death.
  - Nero—a man who declared, "It is not lawful for Christians to exist."
  - Nero—a man who not only persecuted Christians but who crucified them and lit them as human torches along the streets and byways of Rome.

To all that be in Rome:
- I do not know your names individually.
- I have never been in your homes.
- I have never been in your worship nor preached in your prayer meeting.

But I write to you all because I know. . . .
- I know that you are living at the seat of imperial power.
- I know that you are at the command post of everything which moves against the name of Christ.
- I know that you live in a land where the state has declared that
  - The church will crumble, and
  - Deacons will die, and
  - Singers will be silenced, and
  - Preachers will perish.
- I know that—all for the cause of Christ—you are living in the dungeons of death and the catacombs of human corpses.
- I know that—all for the cause of Christ—you are marching like Christians soldiers on your way to dusty death in the Roman Colosseum.

But, says Paul, I am writing "to all that be in Rome."
Paul's insistence on addressing those residents at Rome is the assurance we need to affirm that

THE GOSPEL KNOWS ABOUT THE ROME IN WHICH WE ARE LIVING!

The relevance of the gospel is that it addresses our condition:
- The Rome of hunger for some and Weight-Watchers for others.
- The Rome of children killing children.
- The Rome of heroin and cocaine and Herpes and AIDS.

The gospel has our address and is acquainted with where and under what conditions we live.
The gospel speaks to those who are counted among principalities and powers; those who sit in high places of

governmental authority and who do not want the church to survive.

The gospel—the Good News—is possessed of a sensitivity to
- Pain and poverty,
- Sickness and sadness,
- Destruction and death.

There's just something about the gospel. It doesn't have our name on it and, at the same time, our name is written all over it.

There's just something about the gospel. It counts every hair on your head, and it knows when we dash our foot against a stone.

There's just something about the gospel. It feeds us and clothes us and cleanses us.

And every once in a while God grabs hold of a gospel preacher and provides a gospel message.

And sometimes God writes it down in a gospel letter and sends you word that, no matter how heavy the burden, God knows how much you can bear!

I say, every once in a while God grabs hold of a gospel preacher and provides a Good News message so much so that even though he's preaching to thousands you walk away saying: "He preached that sermon just for me!"

Every once in a while God sends a word with your name on it, but it's not just for you; it's really "to all that be in Rome."

Examine this text again and you will discover that Paul sent his letter "to all that be in Rome, *beloved of God.*"

What a word for those who were the outcasts of the social order—to know that they were the beloved of God.

What a word! Although ostracized by fellow Jews of their own rank and station they are called by Paul "beloved of God."

Have you ever pondered, have you ever stopped to think, what it was that sustained those Christians of the early church?
- They had no money.
- They had no social standing.
- They had no political power.

▪ They had no large numbers following in their ranks.

The only thing they had to sustain them, the only thing they had to give them hope, was an abiding confidence in the abiding, abundant love of God.

And, like it or not, that's all we've got.

▪ We don't really have any money.

▪ We don't really have social standing or status.

▪ We don't have political power.

▪ We don't have anything to put our name on the front page of the newspaper. But we are the beloved of God.

> Behold what manner of love
> the father hath bestowed upon us,
> that we should be called
> the sons [and daughters] of God.

Called to Be Saints

But all this is really nothing new. These lines over which we have come are but standard fare in all Paul's letters. Quite so. But the thing which disturbed me and disturbs me still is that Paul sent his letter to those who were "called to be saints."

My problem is that

▪ I know that I am a citizen of a contemporary Rome—and so Paul's "Rome" includes me.

▪ I know that I am among the beloved of God and so God's love includes me.

But what disturbs me is this being called to be a *saint*. Consequently, I'm not so sure this letter has my name on it.

Every Child of God Has Been Called

What Paul may be saying is that just as he has acknowledged that *he* has been called, every child of God also has been called.

Even though the preacher must be "called," every child of God must be "called" to minister and to ministry as well. The "call" is the sign and symbol of God's benediction upon the ministry as well as the assurance of God's blessings upon it. Consequently, if there is no benediction, there is no blessing.

One must teach within the Christian community because God has called one to teach.

One must minister through music and sing because God has made it one's calling.

One must serve the missionary causes of the church because God has ordained it and because God has called you into being for this ministry.

And that which God has called into being, God blesses.

The Importance of What You Call Yourself

Again, what Paul may be suggesting here is that who you are (your own sense of self-identity) is often revealed by what you call yourself. The name you call yourself is indicative not only of self-perception but of personal value and worth.

It's one thing to call yourself a teacher, but you go to another level when you call yourself an educator.

It's one thing to call yourself a cook, but you go to another level when you call yourself a caterer or a chef.

It's one thing when you call yourself a banker, but you go to another level when you call yourself a financier.

You are what you think you are. You are what you perceive yourself to be. You are becoming what you are in the moment you speak the words which identify how you are to be "called."

Paul simply says that even though you are "in Rome," you are the "beloved of God," but you are also called to be *somebody*, you are "called to be saints!"

The Definition of a Saint

Saint? I am more than a little worried about this *saint* business.

- Does this mean that if I am a saint that I have to be free from sin?
- Does this mean that if I am a saint that I must be "holier-than-thou"?

- Does this mean that if I am a saint I must wear my own personalized holy halo?

The answer to these questions is no!

A saint is one who is being made holy by the presence of the Holy Spirit in his life. A saint is one who is being made holy by the pervasive power and influence of Jesus Christ on both character and conduct. The result is that if Jesus Christ has claimed your life, *you are a saint!*

- A part of the holy nation.
- A part of the royal priesthood.
- A part of the peculiar people.
- Counted among the elect of God.

It is not just a description of what you do; it is the name by which you are known and called: You are a saint!

And you never thought of yourself as a saint?! I must tell you that you cannot be "in Christ" and not be a saint. Not only that, you cannot be in the church and not be in the company of the saints. Paul writes of it over and over again.

First Corinthians says that we must not take our internal church problems to the courts; we must take them before the saints.

Ephesians says that the work of the church is to edify the body of Christ and to perfect the saints.

Ephesians also says that even when you pray, you must pray with all perseverance and supplication "for all the saints."

First Thessalonians says that when Jesus comes again, he's coming for all his saints.

Jude says that we must contend for the faith once delivered to the saints.

The Scriptures verify that, indeed, we are the saints of God.

Some years ago I remember hearing my father, pastor of the Mount Olivet Church in Columbus, Ohio, for more than three decades, deal with this issue of who is and who is not a saint. I shall never forget his own private and personal definition of a saint:

28

A SAINT IS NOTHING BUT A SINNER WHO KEEPS ON STRUGGLING!

And that is why you can look to your right and to your left and say "Good morning" to a saint!

How Saints Get to Be Saints

To be a saint is an awesome claim and calling. This notion of our being *saints* puts us in with some mighty high-class folks. It means, perhaps, that I can stand on the same footing with St. Thomas Aquinas and St. Augustine and St. Bonaventure and St. Francis of Assisi, and St. Theresa of Avila, not to mention St. Matthew, St. Mark, St. John, St. Peter, St. Paul, and all the rest.

While researching this matter of how saints get to be saints, I discovered that there are, according to the Holy Catholic Church, at least two criteria for sainthood.

1. You must be eligible for the process of beatification.

Beatification simply means that you have been blessed. I suppose that means I'm qualified.
   - I had food on my table this morning—I'm blessed.
   - I had clothes to put on—I'm blessed.
   - I was reared by a gospel preacher and a praying mother— I'm blessed.

Everywhere I turn there is evidence that I'm blessed. How about you? Can't you count your blessings?

> Count your blessings—name them one by one;
> Count your blessings—see what God has done!

More than this, I discovered a second requirement for sainthood.

2. There must be two miracles associated with that person's life.

Are there any miracles in your life? Oh, they may not be miracles of the supernatural, they may not be miracles which cannot be explained by scientific method, but they are miracles nonetheless. Perhaps the miracles in your life are like the miracles in mine:

- I've seen three children born in this world—that's a miracle.
- I've gone under a surgeon's knife, and ether had me somewhere between life and death, but I'm here—that's a miracle.
- I've seen men and women come down the aisle of the church with lives changed—that's a miracle.

All you need to do is look around you, and the evidence of miracles is there in abundance.

You have been blessed. You have had more than one miracle in your life. You qualify. You meet the criterion. You are a saint!

> Oh, when the saints go marching in.
> Oh, when the saints go marching in.
> Oh, Lord, I want to be in that number
> When the saints go marching in!

EPILOGUE

Tarsus

To my beloved son and brother in the faith:

Grace and peace from God our Father and our Lord Jesus Christ. Beecher, God as my witness, I make mention of you constantly in my prayers these days requesting that I might by some means be able to journey to see and to hear a word about your mission. There are some spiritual gifts I want to impart to you, even as I have to many others. Reading your epistle, even the word which you preach, to those called to be saints at Washington, I thank my God for the faith I see evident among you.

Your message was delivered to me here, and I am filled with humility for the credence you give to my words sent so long ago to my fellow-sufferers at Rome. My words were intended,

Beecher, for saints living after the resurrection and for all that would hear the word of our Lord Jesus Christ — first to the Jew and then to the Greek. Called to be apostles, we must faint not in our mission to spread the gospel throughout all nations.

I thank God for those called to be saints at Washington and within the community of Christians you serve called Metropolitan. They, too, are constant in my prayers. Though I have not journeyed to Washington — indeed, though I knew nothing about it — you, my beloved son, along with many other preachers and pastors, have taken my words (they are the words of our Father) there for me. I thank my God for your belief in my writings on the Good News of Jesus Christ.

Do not fear to use my writing in your preaching. We who are called to be apostles are of one body in Christ. While I cannot be with you in this season, my words — given me by our Lord and entrusted to me because of the power of his resurrection — are able to endure for preaching in season and out. Let those called to be saints share these words and speak these words openly that all people may hear, those who are aware of the living Christ and those who still are unaware, the Jew and the Greek and the Gentile (those old divisions Christ came to abolish). Exclude no one. My words were directed to the church at Rome; but they are no less and no more for the hearing of those in the faith and out.

We must always firmly establish ourselves in the faith for the sake of our mission, Beecher. In writing to Rome — an unknown church to me — it was necessary to set myself as the deliverer of the word, the writer of the epistle, the evangelist telling the saints of the drama of salvation. Even now more so must we speak of the sacrifice of our Lord and Savior Jesus Christ at Calvary. In so doing, I affirm my servanthood to Jesus, even my enslavement to that servitude. More so than ever I know that I am that slave. I am that servant. I am called to be an apostle.

My son, the word you speak is true. There can be no question in the minds of those called to be saints. God must establish in our minds through faith, not only who I am or who you are, but who we must be and who we must become. If our calling is genuine then our words of preaching to them will have new meaning and will provide new direction. We must become in our bodies the Word we preach with our mouths. When this harmony shall come to pass, the people will know it and rejoice.

I have labored long over your word of preaching, Beecher. As it is sometimes difficult for you to understand my word, I have experienced the same difficulty understanding your own. There is something peculiar about the preaching of the gospel which even now I do not fully understand. As even you have written, "There is something about the gospel that suits your case when the preacher can't call your name." I pondered long on these words, Beecher, and I say to you that those called to be saints have names — common names in the body of Christ: saints, Christians, children. My name is Apostle. My name is Christian. My name is Preacher, and I am called to that witness of my faith. This too was your meaning, as much as I perceive it.

Those at Rome were unknown to me, (as are those at Washington and at Metropolitan), but I know what you and other fellow-sufferers of the gospel are bearing for the sake of Christ. Our faith does not protect us from human death in the body. Rather, our faith gives us new life after death because of the resurrection of Jesus.

Beecher, who is the Nero in your region? Who says now that it is not lawful for Christians to exist? Could it be the plague of men and women in flight — in flight from their faith in God to renew their spirits, to assure their salvation? Let all men and women know assuredly that the word of truth must be spoken where you are, Beecher. It must be spoken in bold and uncompromising tones that all may hear and live.

In meditation and prayer I wrote to Rome lest things of the flesh o'ershadow things of the heart. Tell Washington, Beecher, what matters is not slavish obedience to the laws of men but willing obedience to the laws of God. Tell all the cities of your region — Jew and Gentile — that God is no respecter of persons; all are equal in the searching and seeking eyes of God.

As you well know, I am a circumcised Jew, converted, a former slave of the law, a Pharisee, but converted on the road to Damascus. I started on the road to kill Christians — but what began as a destiny of death became a lifetime of discipleship. No man believed me at the first. It is always difficult for those of the world to comprehend the complete change which occurs in those who are in Christ. Consequently, my own kinsman rose up to slay me. But the Lord sent Barnabas to be by my side. He has helped me even as I now want to help you.

Be cautious, my son. Not all those with whom you come into contact are saints. Many will feign their saintliness. Likewise all are not called to be apostles. Many will feign their apostolic calling. Let them hear the Word and, in faith, be doers of the Word. You are called to preach the Word. As I have written: how shall they hear without a preacher?

To those who are called to be saints and to you whom they know as apostle — your words are worthy of the gospel we preach. Saint is not just a description of what you do; it is what you do upon hearing and believing and accepting the love of Christ. That is what makes us worthy of the name of saints.

Be steadfast in your preaching to the saints in Washington and everywhere, my son, because Rome is everywhere and Nero is everywhere and Jesus is everywhere too.

Grace and peace of our Lord Jesus Christ be with you alway.

>Your father and brother in the faith,
>Paul

2

THE POWER TO PREACH

PROLOGUE

Washington, D.C.

Dear Paul:

Thank you for answering my letter and for sharing with me regarding the saints. I must be honest—I really didn't think that you would write back. We are so different, you and I, and we really are worlds apart. More than that, you know how we preachers can get sometimes—get a few letters from our "fans," and we become too big for our britches! I don't know if you experienced it in your day, but we now have enormous churches with preachers who are far too busy to fellowship with other preachers. We call such churches "mega-churches" (by which we mean that they have over five thousand members or are too fancy to have an ol' fashioned prayer meeting). I confess that we preachers are often not the supportive <u>koinonia</u> we should be. But preachers really do need to talk to preachers. So thanks for writing back!

Paul, I have a serious question to ask, and I hope that you will not be aggravated by its seeming impertinence. Do you ever wish you had never been called? I mean, wouldn't you have preferred to have an "average," "normal" Christian life, without this nagging,

gnawing feeling that for some reason God is using you
to declare his Word and to speak his truth?

You see, I have to confess that sometimes I am
irritated and aggravated by my "call" to preach. First of
all, it's hard to define what it is, and whenever you do,
people look at you as if you're strange—as though you
may be the visiting preacher from Pluto. Even if you
define it, you are forever running out of the resources
necessary to be faithful to it.

Our preaching, Paul, is under different circumstances, but let me share with you the questions which
preaching has occasioned for me.

Why would God choose preaching as his instrument? Surely he could have designed a more effec-
tive and convenient means of achieving his purposes.

Why would God use those whom he knows are
flawed, those who have been touched and tainted by
sin and Satan?

Why would God use those who are often unable to
bring the multiple needs of mind and body under
subjection (as you call it) and expect them to speak
an authentic word to others who are suffering the
same malady?

By what means do we ask others to understand
who and what we are? There is nothing normative
about this business of being a preacher. Just as in
your day when the Saduccees and the Pharisees and
the scribes, the elders and the Essenes were the
order of the day, now we are conservative and lib-
eral, evangelical and reformed. Some churches have
bishops, others do not. Some turn their collars
backward or wear funny little pointed hats, and believe it or not, some of them are women!

Help, Paul! What's a preacher supposed to be?
What's a preacher supposed to look like? They voted me

out of the Minister's Conference because I don't think I have the right to tell God whom he can and cannot call. What's a preacher to do?

You can imagine what has happened as a result of this great diversity. In some respects it has brought a richness to the ministry and has enabled us to reach many because of our priestly pluralism. At the same time, because there are so few standards and so little that is normative for us, many have lost respect for preachers, and I suspect that many preachers have lost respect for themselves.

Then there's the problem of weakness. Not sin, not wickedness, just weakness, a power failure. I'm taking about the need to have the power to do what it is we are called to do and to do it with the dynamic force which it demands. Where do we find that power, Paul? You have suggested strongly that the power we need and seek is to be found in the gospel of Jesus Christ itself. More than that, if I am reading you correctly, you believe that the power to preach not only infects the preacher, but it has a redeeming and saving power over those who are nearby to listen and to hear.

Well, I don't always have that power Paul. Sometimes even when I sit to listen to what God would have me say, I don't feel that power. When I try to put pen to paper and record for myself and for others what I am led of the Spirit to share, I don't always sense that power. Sometimes I'm walking from my office (Paul I know you never had an office and sometimes I wish I didn't. It's a place where preachers get trapped so that people don't have to go hunting them down.) ... Sometimes I'm walking from my office to the pulpit, and I am so weak and so drained and so convinced that I don't have the power that the last thing I want to do is preach. And yet I must preach. I have no choice in the matter. It is an aggravating and infuriating thing— this business called preaching.

Last week I tried to share with our congregation some of my inner thoughts on this business of preaching and the need to have power to do it. I know how important preaching was for you and how much you wanted to preach the gospel in Rome. So I'm sending along another of my sermons. Read it in your spare time and then let me know how preachers can find what I call the power to preach.

Thanks for listening and sharing.

Grace and peace!
Beecher

Sermon: THE POWER TO PREACH

So, as much as in me is, I am ready to preach the gospel to you that are at Rome also. For I am not ashamed of the gospel of Christ: for it is the power of God unto salvation to every one that believeth; to the Jew first, and also to the Greek (Romans 1:15–16).

Even the most casual observer is able to discover in the apostle Paul his longing to make a "pastoral call" on that first-century church situated in that ancient city called Rome. I do not know why Paul was so enamored with Rome. I cannot tell you why Paul had such a burning desire to visit that city set on seven hills. There is no question but that Paul's desire to preach in Rome far exceeded his desire to preach at Philippi, surpassed his yen to preach at the thriving seaport at Thessalonica and went beyond his need to address the residents of Athens, the intellectual capital of the civilized world. In spite of all of Paul's travels, from the Cicilian gates to the Egnatian Way, his greatest desire, his greatest determination and destination was to stand in the City of the Caesars—to stand in that city of architectural splendor and governmental power—Paul's greatest dream was to declare God's word in that city called Rome.

You are aware then that when Paul writes the opening lines of his letter to the church at Rome his dream of visiting there is as yet unrealized. Paul introduces himself and declares

37

that he is "a servant of Jesus Christ, called to be an apostle, separated unto the Gospel of God." Paul makes it clear to whom he is writing—the "beloved of God, called to be saints." Paul then tells his readers of his remorse at not being able to come to Rome. He offers his words of appropriate thanksgiving when he reminds his readers that he is "debtor both to the Greeks and to the Barbarians; both to the wise, and to the unwise." But then, having said all of that, Paul comes to the essence of this word:

> So, as much as in me is,
> I am ready to preach the gospel
> to you that are at Rome also.
> For I am not ashamed of the gospel of Christ:
> for it is the power of God unto salvation
> to everyone that believeth.

Ready to Preach

It is not difficult to dissect or to digest this word for, in reality it speaks plainly for itself. Paul says, "I am ready to preach the gospel!"

Perhaps there is more than the suggestion here that it may take some time simply for a preacher to be *ready* to preach.

Having been "in church" all of one's life does not mean that one is ready to preach.

The fact that one has attended the local seminary or is a holder of theological degrees is no assurance that one is ready to preach.

And stumbling upon a fairly decent sermon every Sunday or so still does not mean that one is ready to preach.

The lesson is clear: one does not get *ready* to preach over night. The example of the apostle Paul is instructive. Paul says, by means of an unwritten "Now":

- After my seminary training at the feet of Gamaliel, now . . .

- After a siege of temporary blindness on the road to Damascus, now . . .

- After having my name changed and my identity altered, now . . .
- After having escaped Damascus in a basket, now . . .
- After having been given this thorn in the flesh, this agent of Satan to buffet me, now . . .
- After having been in jail and holding a prayer meeting with Silas that caused an earthquake in Philippi, now . . .
- After all of this . . . after all of my ups and downs, my trials and tribulations, my poverty and my plenty, my feasting and my famine, . . . *now* I am *ready* to preach the gospel!

I assure you that I am painfully and personally aware that a preacher is not always ready to preach. More than twelve years ago the Lord placed me in the pulpit of the Metropolitan Church and gave me a congregation to preach to even if I didn't have much to preach. I had a desire to say something; I just needed something to say! It is only now after the experience of these years, however, that I know that the Lord himself will get a preacher ready to preach.

- It takes some long meetings, but he will get you ready to preach.
- It takes some disappointments, but he will get you ready to preach.
- It takes ridicule and rejection, but he will get you ready to preach.
- It takes briny tears, and sometimes it takes a wrestling match with your pillow all night long, but he will get you ready to preach.
- It takes those things that send you to your knees in order to get you on your feet, but he will get you ready to preach. That is why every preacher touched by the cleansing, purifying, sanctifying fire of God comes to that moment when he or she is able to say along with Paul, "I am ready to preach the gospel."

Looking at this word again one discovers that when Paul says, "I am ready to preach the gospel," he does not use the Greek *kerygma*, usually translated "to preach." Rather, he uses the Greek *euangelizo* which means not only "to evangelize," but to proclaim the Good News concerning the Son of God. The implication is that when we preach the gospel—the *euangelizo* —we become the *euangelilon*, the messenger who brings good news.

There is yet another word directly related to *euangelilon: evangelos*. James W. Cox in his book *Preaching* has instructed that the *evangelos* is the soldier who comes from the field of battle (whether by ship or by horse or on foot) with a leafy garland about his head, races into the city with hands raised, and cries out, "*Chaire, nikomen!*" or "Greetings! We have won!" That's good news! A clearer understanding of what Paul is saying is:

- I am ready to preach the gospel.
- I am ready to be the *evangelos*.
- I am ready to tell you that we have won!

What a word from an imprisoned preacher sitting in a jail cell sent to church folk hiding out in caves and catacombs whose condition and disposition are the very definition of doom and defeat. What a word: We have won!

What a word from a limping, itinerant Jewish preacher on his way to Nero's chopping block along with those to whom he wrote: We have won!

What a word from a nearly blind, shivering, lonely, forsaken, worn out, burned out, and stressed-out preacher given to those who would soon make their way into the Roman Colosseum to become food for lions: We have won!

What a word from one who had spent twenty-three years on three missionary journeys establishing churches all over Asia Minor and had seen churches divided over doctrine, fractured by jealousy and envy and pettiness and strife, set upon by Satan, infiltrated by preachers who were impostors, rocked by the sexual scandal of incest in the church, and yet could still declare Good News: We have won!

Paul's example is, in fact, the definition of authentic preaching. The preacher, the *evangelos*, is to tell those who have been

- Dejected and deserted,
- Deceived and deflated,
- Defiled and degraded,
- Demoralized and defeated

that there is Good News: We have won!

The Power of the Preacher and Preaching

One must not forget that the preacher has been given *power over sickness*. When sickness has done its work and the doctors have shaken their heads and turned away, that's the time for the *evangelos* to say a word about a "Doctor that has never lost a patient." That's the time for the *evangelos* to say a word about a Doctor that still makes "house calls." That's the time for the *evangelos* to step in and say, despite all odds and all depressing diagnosis, there is Good News: We have won!

One must not forget that the preacher has been given *power over unclean spirits*. When Satan has done his or her work, when Satan has walked up and down in the earth seeking to devour, when the demons of modern life cause neurosis and psychosis, that is the time for the preacher to "bind" Satan in the name of Jesus. That is the time for the preacher, in the words of our forefathers, to talk about a "heart fixer and a mind regulator." And when the "Legions" of this world are clothed and in their right minds, that's the time to run with the Good News: We have won!

There is, I am confident, strange power in this preaching business. Year after year, century upon century, preachers have been preaching. Very often it's the same preacher, preaching the same sermon about the same Jesus, the same crucifixion, and the same resurrection. Is it not so that even though the preacher tells the same story in the same way Sunday after Sunday men and women still keep coming back to hear it over again? Evidently there is strange power in the business of preaching. The question is, what is this power, why this power, and how is it manifest?

In the first instance there is power in preaching because

THE POWER TO PREACH

The activity in our world, the activity in our lives requires that each of us stop to ask, "Where am I?" To overstate the obvious is to suggest that in order to find out whether you are lost you must first discover where you are. Somehow the gospel helps us fix our location. We hear a sermon that describes our condition and our situation, and strangely enough it helps bring definition to where we are and clarity to what we are experiencing. It fixes our location when, in response to the preaching of the gospel, we are able to say, "That's me!"

If you identify with *the woman with an issue of blood*, perhaps it means that you too have been sick and unable to recover. Because you are empathetic with her condition of loneliness and helplessness and have seen that same condition in your own experience that enables you to say, "That's me," it helps you to know where you are.

If you identify with *the man born blind* and suddenly you realize that there are some things you can't see, when you become aware of the blindness that causes you to stumble in the darkness and when you find yourself feeling your way along the blackened corridors of a sunless society, and when you realize that, in every respect, you are the man born blind, that too helps you to know where you are.

If you identify with *the prodigal son* (or daughter) and come to the realization that you have spent your inheritance in riotous, unproductive, unredemptive living; if you are able to honestly admit, as a result of hearing again this worn-out parable, that you have also let money run through your fingers like water; if you are able to see that even though you may live in a physical palace you actually reside in a spiritual pigpen; if you are able at least to gain a vision of what you have become realistically, you may not like it, but it helps you to know where you are.

The gospel will help you to know where you are. It's helpful to know where you are. It's important to know when you're lost. It is obviously true that one cannot appreciate being found until one has first been lost. It is precisely in the process of discovering where we are, of moving from lostness to foundness that there comes new meaning to old words:

> Amazing grace, how sweet the sound,
> That saved a wretch like me.
> I once was lost but now I'm found,
> 'Twas blind but now I see.

In the second instance,

THE GOSPEL HAS THE POWER TO CREATE WHOLE PERSONS IN A BROKEN WORLD.

By and large, the society in which we live has fractured the human personality. Men and women at every turn are seeking to discover how they can become complete persons, preserve the integrity of their individuality and, in a word, become whole. Christian doctrine suggests that we ought to be "in the world but not of the world." That is easier said than done.

Just the other day I discovered a book entitled *How to Be a Plan A Person in a Plan B World*. Robert Schuller has written a book entitled *Self-Esteem: The New Reformation*. Similarly, Denis Waitley has suggested that *Being the Best*, the title of his new book, is the only alternative when the self-help myths leave one empty and hungry for the truth. I am convinced that these books were written simply because a world that specializes in dehumanization ultimately reaps the harvest of persons who have lost all sense of personal dignity and who have become but shattered fragments of a silicon society.

It is in this context that the preaching of the gospel is designed to take the fragments of human life and bring new meaning and new life out of the old.

The preaching of the gospel is designed to take the broken pieces that have sometimes been cast away at the potter's wheel and remake them according to the purposes of the eternal.

The preaching of the gospel is designed to take the wrecked and ruined lives of the culture and subject them to the redemptive and restorative power of the Holy Spirit.

The preaching of the gospel creates whole persons in a broken world.

- Newlyweds at Cana, what happened to you?
  "He took our water and turned it into wine!"
- Young man with a withered hand, what happened to you?
  "He straightened out my hand and then he straightened out my life!"
- Ten lepers, what did he do for you?
  "We looked at our hands and they looked new.
  "We looked at our feet and they did too!"
- Man at Bethesda pool, what did he do?
  "He made me stand on my feet, and now my bed no longer carries me; I carry it!"

The preaching of the gospel has the capacity and the power to make persons complete, to make persons whole. At every turn the Scriptures affirm the wholeness which comes through the gospel as manifest in Jesus Christ.

- The Syro-Phoenician woman's daughter was not just healed—she was made whole.
- The centurion's servant was not just healed—he was made whole.
- Jairus' daughter was not just raised from the dead—she was made whole.
- That woman with an issue of blood didn't simply stop bleeding—she was made whole.

Whole! Whole, I say! The gospel makes one whole.

- Jesus said: "You shall know the truth and truth shall set you free."
  When one is free, one is whole!
- Jesus said: "I am come that you might have life and that you might have it more abundantly."
  When one comes to know the abundant life, one is whole!
- Jesus said to those whom he healed: "Go in peace, thy faith hath made thee whole."
  When we discover in the self the capacity for individual faith to produce the individual and psychic capacity for wellness, when we realize through Christ that we have been given stewardship over our lives and our well-

being, we are free, then we are alive, we are whole. And the preaching of the gospel has the capacity to create whole persons in a broken and fragmented world.

In the third instance,

THE GOSPEL IS GOD'S ANSWER TO A BAD REPUTATION!

It has always amazed me, as I have made my way through the Bible, that most of the people with whom the Bible has to deal are themselves faced with the problem of a bad reputation. Don't you find it strange that the book which points persons to righteousness uses as its primary examples men and women who are noted for their unrighteousness? On every page there is somebody with a bad reputation:

- Cain killed Abel.
- Jacob cheated Isaac.
- Moses killed an Egyptian.
- Noah got drunk.
- Baalam was disobedient.
- Samson chose the wrong wife.
- Solomon had too many wives.
- David stole another man's wife.
- Peter was unpredictable.
- Matthew was an extortioner.
- James and John were hotheads.
- Simon was a revolutionary.
- Mark was a cop-out.
- Timothy was a failure.
- Judas was a cheapskate and a thief.

Still the gospel is God's answer to a bad reputation. The gospel is here to let us know that no one is

- Too lost to be found,
- Too low down to be lifted,
- Too far out to be brought in,
- Too dirty to be washed,
- Too hungry to be filled,
- Too thirsty to be satisfied,
- Too soiled to be saved,

- Too repulsive to be redeemed, or
- Too endangered to be rescued.

God himself knows what it is to live with a bad reputation. That's why, one night in Bethlehem, he came down through forty-two generations and, in a manger filled with hay,

> made himself of no reputation, and took upon him the form of a servant, and was made in the likeness of men (Philippians 2:7).

Isaiah said the Savior's reputation was so bad that he was

> despised and rejected of men; a man of sorrows, and acquainted with grief. . . . stricken, smitten, . . . and afflicted. . . . He was wounded for our transgressions, he was bruised for our iniquities: the chastisement of our peace was upon him; and with his stripes we are healed (Isaiah 53:3–5).

God knows what it is to live with a bad reputation. That is why he sits in pigpens with prodigals. That's why he sits on death row in criminals' cells. You'll find him down on the Jericho road where men have been beaten and left for dead. You'll find him on Calvary where he who knew no sin became sin—all because the gospel is God's answer to a bad reputation.

Paul says, "I am ready to preach the gospel." Then this itinerant preacher from Tarsus gives us the reason. He say, "I am ready to preach the gospel . . . for I am not ashamed of the gospel of Christ."

Listen to what Paul says: "Even though Rome is hostile to the very message I bring, I will not creep into Rome under the cloak of anonymity—I am not ashamed of the gospel."

Time and again, Paul says that he has no personal qualities that would gain respect. He is no orator. He is short of stature, bald, and unattractive. He is no preacher of rare or precious gifts. He is no prince of the pulpit with strange or peculiar power above mortal men. And yet, Paul dares to say, "I am not ashamed of the gospel."

Paul would stand in Rome, as well he might, preaching of One who came as the son of a carpenter and who died in the company of criminals. And yet, for all that he had against him,

Paul was confident that there was something else at work for him. That is why he declared, "I am not ashamed of the gospel."

Paul is not ashamed of the gospel, nor should we be, because it is the power of God. It is not *a* power; it is *the* power. The gospel is the *dunamis,* the strength, the dominion, the authority of God, and it assures his salvific work to every one that believes on him.

I stand with Paul. I stand in search of that power to preach. In whatever church, great or small, I seek the power to preach. Without script or purse, cloak or coat, I seek the power to preach. It is with this power that we shall be obedient to his ultimate and final command:

> Go preach my gospel, saith the Lord,
> Bid the whole earth my grace receive;
> He shall be saved that trusts my word,
> And he condemned who'll not believe.
>
> Teach all the nations my commands;
> I'm with you till the world shall end.
> All power is trusted in my hands;
> I can destroy, and I defend.
>
> He spake, and light shone 'round his head;
> On a bright cloud to heaven he rode;
> They to the farthest nations spread
> The grace of their ascended God.

EPILOGUE

Corinth

Beecher, my son and brother in the faith:

You are truly in my prayers this day and always. Each message that I receive from you gives me greater strength to do a greater task for a greater purpose — salvation for mankind. Grace and peace from our Lord Jesus Christ to you and to the family of saints at Washington and at Metropolitan. God has blessed you with the power of his calling, Beecher, and the Power that calls is the Power that preaches, for ultimately he is our Power.

I want to impart some spiritual advice to you, my son, for your meditation and spiritual growth in Christ. Before I do, however, I must ask you if you notice my words and how I am using them in your letters now. I smile when I do so, Beecher, because I am becoming more and more akin to your way with words. If Alexander was a coppersmith, you are becoming something of a "wordsmith" I suspect. I trust that line brought a smile to your face. Don't take yourself so seriously, my son! It is something a little short of miraculous how words grow and change and yet <u>meaning</u> remains constant — Jesus is our salvation.

Your epistle "The Power to Preach" was of great interest to me, and I appreciate your helping me to see how my writings, which some suggest are divinely inspired, have occasioned some inspiration in you.

Beecher, the preacher who never experiences "power failure," as you call it, is one whose power is never used or whose power was in short supply in the first place. The purpose of the power is to use it and to be used by it until we are forced to return to the power source. Did you get a copy of my letter to the Corinthians — or was it Ephesians — where I told the preachers there that our weakness is made perfect in him, or something to that effect.

However, your letter and your questions brought about some questions of my own, and I need to share them with you. This "power to preach," Beecher, was there some private reason that compelled you to speak to the saints about our power? Or was there some question about preaching and power which caused you to do so? How easily you seem to equate preaching and power. Do you presume that one is predicated upon or dictated by the other?

As God is my witness, we can speak with honesty here, Beecher. The integrity of our correspondence is intact; I share it with none other. We are called to be apostles, and this calling places us in spiritual union one with another. I have read with interest your questions, but is there something more beneath the surface, something you are not yet sharing with me, which has caused in you more than ordinary anxiety about your power to preach?

Let me remind you, my son, there was no seminary such as the one you attended where salvation could be gained or where theology could be explored on the road to Damascus. It is true that my seminary professor (a rigid Pharisee named Gamaliel) taught me well the Jewish law, but there was no resurrection and no salvation in the law as we knew it. Neither was there a preaching or homiletics or hermeneutics course at Jerusalem for me, Beecher. I was a Pharisee, a Jew who persecuted Christians. But, Beecher, I do not question my power, my preaching, nor do I measure the power of my preaching by how many are called to be saints upon hearing. Rather, as it is written, I move from faith to faith. Before faith I was confused and confined under the law — restrained, Beecher, in darkness. The law was my custodian and my schoolmaster and there was no justifcation for my belief in the law except that I was the product of my environment and my teaching.

As I get older it becomes increasingly difficult to remember where I said things or when I wrote them, but I distinctly remember writing these words:

> *For God, who commanded the light to shine out of darkness, hath shined in our hearts, to give the light of the knowledge of the glory of God in the face of Jesus Christ.*

Oh, yes, I remember now. It was to those Christians in Corinth that I wrote these words. But I bring them to remembrance now because my power, my preaching power, my urgency and claim of call does not come from within, it comes from without. The validation of what I do and what I say comes alone from him who is the source and author of all power. When I think of Jesus and the power of his resurrection, it not only gives me power, it gives me the authority to preach. Remember, Beecher, we preach not ourselves but Jesus Christ. He alone calls us and claims us and impregnates us with his power to preach his Word to his people.

Write again, soon, Beecher. By the way, sometimes your sermons infuriate me, because I think you have cleaned them up. Don't forget that I am a preacher also and I know when the "good stuff" has been left out. Let me have it. I can take it. God be praised for the ministry of preaching the glorious gospel of Jesus Christ which he has given to me and to you also.

Pax vobiscum,
Paul

P.S.: If you ever give up on your power to preach and leave the pulpit for good, come over to see me and I will teach you how to make tents!

3

FROM FAITH TO FAITH

PROLOGUE

Washington, D.C.

Dear Paul:

Your suggestion that perhaps I need to learn how to make tents may be more apt than you realized. The value, as you know, of living in a tent is that you are housed in a portable structure. You are never tied down to one spot, always free to move at a moment's notice. To live and to minister in the closing moments of the twentieth century is to live in a world where such freedom of movement is essential. This is primarily so because everything around us is moving. It is as though nothing is stable, nothing is permanent, everything is in a perpetual state of motion and flux.

I've had a notion recently that perhaps the true calling of the church is be a spiritual refugee camp for people in a perpetual state of transition from one spiritual war to another, always living in tents and always on the move. I am not yet convinced that the church Jesus had in mind was intended to be stiff and stationary. Perhaps—and it's just a fleeting thought—the one who taught in cornfields and preached on hillsides really wanted us to have portable pulpits and transient temples. So don't be surprised, Paul, if I take you up on your tent-making lessons.

By the way, what kind of letters are these anyway? Sometimes I feel as though I am on a psychiatrist's couch. You seem to have an uncanny way of seeing right through me. You are right. I have been trying to "clean up" these sermons a little. Obviously, not with much success.

You see, I am a part of that generation of preachers that believes that sermons should be what we call "deep" or "heavy" or profound. I am caught between trying to make the sermon read well and sound good. What looks to the eye of the reader to be <u>wordiness</u> takes on a different <u>sound</u> in the pulpit when it gains vocal expression. But in print this wordiness makes what we say seem insignificant, trite. What I really hope to do is to reveal the profound truth hidden in the words. And since I am corresponding and communicating with you, Paul, (speaking on behalf of many other preachers) I don't want to leave you with the impression that all modern preachers are simple-minded.

At the same time that I want to be taken seriously as a thoughtful and profound preacher, I am convinced that the essence of the gospel of Jesus Christ is not to be found in its profundity but in its simplicity. I really want to find in a sermon the balance between what is intellectually grounded, philosophically appropriate, and academically stimulating and what is biblically rich, spiritually inspiring, and nourishing to the whole congregation. I guess what I am looking for, Paul, is that profundity of simplicity that is on the other side of complexity. Perhaps, as our sharing continues, you will be able to help me achieve this sense of balance.

I am still enthralled and enamored with your letter to the Roman Christians. I am particularly interested in understanding how they received your letter.

When I realize that you wrote it to people who were hiding in underground cemeteries and when I see you open up your discussion of justification, it seems to me heady language for a crisis situation. On the other hand, when you began to open up the faith issue it seemed to be the needed word for the times. I'm not really criticizing your methodology Paul, but I am saying that it opened up new questions and new sensitivities about the Christian walk.

The sermon that I am enclosing with this letter is one with which I wrestled a long time. The problem before me was to define what Clarence Jordan called "the substance of faith." It seems to me, Paul, that even you had difficulty defining what faith is. We've been debating whether or not you really wrote the letter to the Hebrews, and if you did, what you meant when you said: "Faith is the substance of things hoped for; the evidence of things not seen."

The need for clarity on this faith issue was never more apparent than in our time. While you had to live with that maniac Nero who sat on the imperial throne of Rome, we must live with other "Neros" who seek to dictate the quality and character of our lives. We have reached the point where our children are not content with their lives and are seeking alternative expressions and solutions in sex and drugs and alcohol. When parents must stand by and watch the destruction of their children, they wonder what could be the value of faith. When the foundations of our basic institutions seem to be crumbling before our eyes and when even the religious enterprise seems rocked by its own instability, it shakes our trust in your concept of faith.

We live in a time, Paul, much like your own, when God seems to have been eradicated from the collective consciousness of our social order. If the truth be known, Paul, we too are citizens of a pagan world— when it appears that all sense of propriety, order, and godliness are gone. With all of this insanity, how can we maintain faith?

While writing this sermon I really wished I could have picked up the telephone and had you dictate a few lines to straighten out my confusion and help my congregation the next morning. I tried to read what Martin Luther had written, but to be honest (and this may be heresy), he seemed a little more confused than the rest of us.

So I tried it Paul—I stepped out on faith. Not knowing what the end would be, I simply began with a serious question, hoping that we would reach a credible ending. I discovered that the writing and the preaching of the sermon was an adventure of faith in and of itself. I do not think of this as a very <u>strong</u> sermon. It is more a wrestling, a grappling, a coming to grips with some hard concepts you have laid before us.

Be charitable with your reading, and especially with your evaluation and response. As ever, you are constantly in my prayers. I hope to hear from you soon.

Your brother in the faith,
Beecher

P.S.: If you teach me how to make tents, I'll teach you how to swing a three iron (something we do in a game called "golf"). You should thank God always that they didn't have golf in your day. If you think you know what faith is, you should try golf!

Sermon: FROM FAITH TO FAITH

For I am not ashamed of the gospel of Christ: for it is the power of God unto salvation to every one that believeth; to the Jew first, and also to the Greek. For therein is the righteousness of God revealed from faith to faith; as it is written, The just shall live by faith (Romans 1:16–17).

The serious student of the Bible would be well advised to engage his or her mind and spirit in an analysis of some text of Scripture which is at once too difficult, too complicated, and seemingly too intricate to understand. I make this rather startling and unorthodox suggestion primarily because, as most prospectors have discovered, golden nuggets are never found on the surface but are usually buried and hidden deeply within the soil. To be sure, that which is to be found on the surface is usually a part of the veneer, the peripheral, and the superficial. But that for which one must dig and search out and inquire and examine usually has value which far exceeds one's expectations. And that is why, I suppose, Jesus suggested that the kingdom of God is really "a treasure hid in a field."

Recently I have been inquiring and digging around the soil of this text imbedded, as it were, within the fertile ground of this first chapter of Romans. Paul, as you know, from his writing table in Corinth, has greeted the saints of God who are among those headed for slaughter in the Roman Colosseum. Paul, now, this aging and yet ageless veteran of many missionary journeys, confirms for them his intention to visit and, not only that, but to preach in Rome, the very seat of the caesars. Having said all of that, however, Paul now comes to his central theme. Having finished the preliminary salutations of his pastoral epistle, Paul now comes to that refrain which will be heard again and again (directly and by implication) throughout the whole of his letter. It is in these few words that one finds the reason that the entire book of Romans was written. Paul says, "For I am not ashamed of the gospel of Christ . . . for therein is *the righteousness of God revealed from faith to faith; as it is written, the just shall live by faith."*

Now, I say, the serious student of the Scriptures will not want to pass these rather uninteresting, intricate, and complicated concepts too swiftly. A look at history reveals that these very words brought on a salvation experience for John Wesley and started a revival that turned the whole nation of England upside down. One might not want to discount these words too quickly. Martin Luther read about this "faith to faith" and "the just shall live by faith" and the whole Protestant Reformation knew its birth.

One might want to just pause at these passages, for here is the birthing and breeding ground of timeless Christian concepts. Here is a word about the nature of salvation and justification and revelation and righteousness and faith. It does not look like it on the surface, but there is some gold here.

There's something of value here. There's something of importance here. And so I thought that with a little searching and inquiring and exegetical examination, we could discover what Paul means when he uses the phrase "from faith to faith" and when he says, "the just shall live by faith."

The Power to Save

Now, at the outset, one ought not to be so taken with the notion that Paul is not ashamed of the gospel. One ought not to be so quick to notice that Paul is ready to preach the gospel without understanding why. Paul says "I am ready to preach the gospel first of all because it is *the power of God unto salvation."*

I assure you I shall not tabernacle here, but I need to stop long enough to tell you that the gospel has the power to save. It's not a very comfortable or contemporary concept, but men still need to be saved.

There is no purpose in the life or the ministry of the church unless somebody is being saved.

There is no point in maintaining these structures of stone we call churches unless somebody is being saved.

There is neither rhyme nor reason to the ceaseless singing of the songs of Zion unless somebody is being saved.

There is no value in preaching unless lives are being changed. Indeed, worship is not worship until someone has been claimed and come forward for Christ.

- Alcoholics need to be saved from slow-death suicide.
- Drug addicts need to be saved from pills and needles and hashish and grass.
- Teenagers need to be saved from throwing their lives away all because of a feeling.
- Our children need to be saved from a society where they are being gunned down in the streets over the insignificant minutia of consumer items they do not need and cannot afford.
- The poor need to be saved from a land of economic death, where crash has become commonplace and where real

depression starts in the pocketbook and then works its way to the mind.

- The hungry need to be saved in a land where fields lie fallow and farmers are given tax incentives not to grow crops while hundreds of thousands die of starvation in the streets.
- Homes need to be saved from internal destruction.
- Churches and church folk need to be saved from the self-deceptive practice of acting one way and living another.

I am convinced that there is no value in preaching if we are not about the business of saving souls. In this connection I am convinced as well that the gospel has the power to save. That is why this same Paul wrote, "If any man be in Christ, he is a new creature: old things are passed away; behold, all things are become new."

Somebody needs to be saved. Preachers must be convinced that he who would declare this word must be content to be a *nobody* who is willing to tell *everybody* that there is *Somebody* who is able to save *anybody!* Paul says he preaches this gospel for one reason—it is the power of God unto salvation. The gospel is preached because it has the power to save.

The Righteousness of God

Let's dig a little deeper. There's more than that. Paul says, *"For therein . . .*—in the gospel, in the Good News, in this word that we preach—*"for therein is the righteousness of God revealed."*

Now, this business of the righteousness of God—what a high and lofty concept. On the surface, it simply serves to underscore the "rightness" of God. But there is a problem with gaining an understanding of this idea of righteousness. For we say that God is always right. And we say that God is always in the right. And we say that God will always do what is right. But the problem is that what is right can only be determined and measured against him who is right.

And so there is more here. The righteousness of God is revealed in the gospel. The righteousness of God is revealed in the New Testament because there is some question about the righteousness of God in the Old Testament. Throughout the whole of the Old Testament there is a lingering question about the character of God—who he is, what he does, and how he provides. On every page of the old Scripture there is a question mark about the nature of God and the activity of God. In the eighteenth chapter of Genesis (18:25) you will discover that even Abraham has a rhetorical question regarding the righteousness of God when he asks, "Shall not the Judge of all the earth do right?"

There is a question about God. Ever since the dawn of creation, when Adam and Eve were evicted as the first tenants of the Eden Garden Condominium Apartments, there's been a question about the justice of God.

Ever since the children of Adam and Eve built their tower of Babel into the heavens and God himself confused their languages, there's been a question about the purpose and intent of God.

Ever since Sodom and Gomorrah and the whole unseemly business of that illicit sex scandal that rocked the church, when even the preacher's wife—you remember the Reverend Doctor Lot—when even she had to be turned into a pillar of salt, there's been some question about God's ability to be God.

Ever since the children of Israel left the slave fields of Egypt for the freedom fields of the Promised Land—and then they fussed and fought for forty years, going round and round for forty years, a two-week journey turned into forty years—ever since that time there have been some questions about God's qualifications to be the leader he claims to be.

Ever since the record was revealed about covenants that were broken and kings that could not rule and judges that could not escape corruption and priests that were killed and prophets that were stoned, there's been some question about God and just what he had in mind for humanity.

Ever since the sin of Adam, there's been some question about how an infinite God can be reconciled to a finite man. There's been some question about how a sinless God would restore his relationship with sinful man. There's been some question about how the gulf would be bridged, the chasm spanned, and the gap closed between a loving God and wayward children. There are just some questions about the righteousness of God.

The result of all these questions about God is that I have some questions of my own. Perhaps you have some questions about the God/man relationship that reaches down to the tap roots of our souls. Perhaps you would be interested to know, if God is all he claims to be.

- How does God propose to fix you when you're broken?
- How does God propose to love you when you're unlovable?
- How does God propose to cleanse you when you're dirty?
- How does God propose to reconcile the irreconcilable?
- How does God propose to make something out of nothing?
- How does God propose to restore the marriage when the divorce has already been decreed?
- How does God, who is Right, propose to take wrong and make wrong right?
- How does God propose to take a crooked pencil and draw straight lines?
- How does God propose to take this messed-up, broken-up, and patched-up life and make it a life worth living?

There are some serious questions about God. But Paul says that if you want to know the answer to these inquiries, the intent of God, the character of God, the nature of God, and the integrity of God, yes, the very righteousness of God, is revealed in the gospel. But then Paul says this righteousness is revealed *"from faith to faith."*

What Faith?

Now, I was having enough trouble trying to understand the righteousness of God, and then Paul said it's from faith to faith. From what faith to what faith? By what means is Paul trying to distinguish one kind of faith from another kind of faith? I'm getting a little confused on this matter of *faith to faith.*

What are the possibilities of Paul's meaning?

▪ It could be that we can only understand the righteousness of God when the faith of the preacher is transmitted and transferred to the faith of the believer.

▪ It could be that we can only understand the righteousness of God when there is a transference from the faith of the Old Testament to the faith of the New Testament.

▪ It could be that Paul is telling his readers that they can only understand the righteousness of God when they make the shift from the faith of Judaism to the faith of Christianity.

▪ It could be that we can only understand the righteousness of God when there is a movement from immaturity to maturity.

▪ It could be that we can only understand the righteousness of God when we step away from that infatuated faith which was ours when we first found the Lord to that faith which comes when we've been through many dangers, toils, and snares.

▪ It could be that we can only understand the righteousness of God when we move from faith in the self to faith in that which is beyond the self. That kind of faith that cries:

> Father, I stretch my hands to thee!
> No other help I know.
> If thou withdraw thyself from me.
> Ah! wither shall I go?

From this preacher's perspective it appears that there is only one way to understand these confusing concepts. There is only one way to come to terms with these perplexing and paradoxical notions of Pauline thought. There is only one way to understand how God and humanity are reconciled. There is only one way to find answers to the ceaseless questions about God's matchless love for mankind. The only way I can tell you (I wish I had something new!) is that . . .

▪ One night, in a little town called Bethlehem, God set out on his great odyssey of redeeming love.

- One night, in spite of man's sin, God came down through forty-and-two generations.
- One night, because of man's sin, God got in touch with a homeless couple, an unwed teenage mother, and a frightened and confused father.
- One night, in the face of man's sin, God shut up the door of an inn so that he would open up the door to eternity.
- One night, God sent his Son, his only Son . . .
  - Sent him to heal the sick, cleanse lepers, still storms, straighten out twisted limbs, unravel knotted tongues, give sight to blinded eyes, unstop deaf ears.
  - Sent him to preach the gospel.
  - Sent him to bring hope to the hopeless.
  - Sent him to accept the unacceptable.
  - Sent him to set captives free.

Just because there were some questions about God . . .
- He sent his Son to take fever out of Peter's mother-in-law.
- He sent his Son to perform psycho-surgery on Legion.
- He sent his Son to take demons out of Mary Magdalene.
- He sent his Son to heal the woman with an issue of blood.

But that's not all he did. If you want to know about the righteousness of God, the character of God, the nature of God, or the integrity of God, I need to tell you that . . .
- One Thursday night, they found him in Gethsemane's garden.
- One Thursday night, they took him to Caiaphas' palace and to Pilate's judgment hall.
- One Thursday night, they took his clothes from him and put on him a purple robe.
- One Thursday night, they put a crown of thorns on his head and then beat him all night long.

But something else must be told if the story is to be complete, and if you want to understand the righteousness of God, righteousness was not defined on Thursday alone. Thursday had to turn into Friday.
- One Friday, they gave him a cross of rough-hewn timber.

- One Friday, they made him carry his cross up the Via Dolorosa.
- One Friday, they nailed him to that cross on the Hill of the Skulls.
- One Friday, they nailed him hand and foot.
- One Friday, they pierced him in the side.

But soon Friday had to live through Saturday in order to get to Sunday. Then it happened!

One Sunday morning, long before the break of day . . .

- One Sunday morning, sad women came to sit watch at the tombstone.
- One Sunday morning, the gardener said, "He is not here but risen, as he said."
- One Sunday morning, he got up with all power in his hand.
- One Sunday morning, he got up with a shout, saying: "Death, where is your victory, Grave, where is you sting?"

And, if you want to know how that takes care of your sin; if you want to know how that washes you; if you want to know how that justifies you; if you want to know how that makes you right with God; if you want to know how that pays your debts and settles your account; if you want to know how that makes the difference in your life, Paul says it happens *from faith to faith*.

The distilled essence of Paul's meaning is this:

You can have the assurance of your salvation, but it's done by faith from beginning to end. You have to start out in faith in order to end up with faith.

- In the morning my faith says that without faith it is impossible to please him.
- And in the evening my faith says that he who cometh to God must believe that he is and that he is a rewarder of them that diligently seek him. That's from faith . . . to faith.

- In the morning my faith says, "Therefore being justified by faith we have peace with God through our Lord Jesus Christ."
- And in the evening my faith says, "God so loved the world, that he gave his only begotten son!" That's from faith . . . to faith.

- In the morning my faith says, "Great is thy faithfulness, O God my father. There is no shadow of turning with thee."
- And in the evening my faith says, "All I have needed thy hand hath provided. Great is thy faithfulness Lord unto me." That's from faith . . . to faith.

- In the morning my faith says, "The Lord is my light and my salvation, whom shall I fear? The Lord is the strength of my life of whom shall I be afraid?"
- And in the evening my faith says, "When mine enemies and my foes come upon me to eat up my flesh they stumbled and fell. Though an host should encamp against me my heart shall not fear." That's from faith . . . to faith.

- In the morning my faith says, "Whatever you ask in my name believing it shall be done."
- And in the evening my faith says, "Ask, and it shall be given; seek, and ye shall find; knock, and the door shall be opened unto you." That's from faith . . . to faith.

In other words, in spite of what happens in my day— sickness, sorrow, unemployment, poverty, famine, distress, depression, desertion, anxiety, burnout, and the rest—in spite of the negativities of human existence, God has fixed it so that the faith with which I begin in the morning of life is the same faith with which I come to rest in the evening of life.

The affirmation we make today is that Paul was right: the just shall live by faith.

We do not live as a result of our possessions; possessions will not last.

We do not live as a consequence of our knowledge; knowledge will vanish away.

We do not live as a beneficiary of social status; fame is fleeting and popularity will pass.

We do not live as a result of our economic investments; "a fool and his money are soon parted."

We will not live because of political party affiliation; God's kingdom is not of this world.

We do not crawl from valley to valley or climb from mountain to mountain on our strength alone; our help is in the Lord who made heaven and earth.

The only way we can live is by faith!

- If you've ever been saved, you can only live by faith.
- If you've ever met the Lord, you can only live by faith.
- If your soul's been converted, you walk by faith and not by sight. The just shall live by faith.

What is faith?

- Faith is Noah building a boat with no water in sight.
- Faith is Moses marching to the Red Sea with no means to get across.
- Faith is three Hebrew boys with no worry on their faces in a fiery furnace.
- Faith is Ezekiel standing to preach in the midst of a cemetery congregation.
- Faith is Job testifying about God's goodness while situated on an ash pile.

Faith says, "My hope is built on nothing less than Jesus' blood and righteousness. I dare not trust the sweetest frame but wholly lean on Jesus' name."

Faith says, "'Tis so sweet to trust in Jesus, just to take him at his word. Just to rest upon his promise. Just to know, Thus saith the Lord.'"

Faith says, "By and by, when the morning come. All the saints of God come gathering home. We will tell the story how we've overcome and we'll understand it better by and by."

You still don't understand the righteousness of God? You're still not quite clear on the meaning of "from faith to faith"? You have still have trouble understanding how it is that the just shall live by faith?

Well, it means . . . just trust him.

- When troubles rise, trust him.
- When the wind blows, trust him.
- When death comes, trust him.
- When you don't have a dime, trust him.
- When you can't make ends meet, trust him.
- When the way gets hard, trust him.
- When friends are few, trust him.
- When you don't see your way, trust him.

Whatever life brings, trust him. Only in this way will you be able to travel from faith . . . to faith!

EPILOGUE

Ephesus

Beecher, my beloved son in the faith:

Grace and peace from God our Father and our Lord Jesus Christ. I thank our God for you, Beecher, and for the comfort of our mutual faith. I am not well in body at this time, and the words of my son and brother in our calling are a light to my life. It is good for those called to be apostles to seek out and care for each other.

I am always grateful for your prayers and keep you constantly in my own and in my heart as well. Through the reading of your preaching I am confident of your faith and of your strength which grows day by day. Be not overcome by the satanic influence of self-doubt; rely upon those spiritual gifts which have come through your parents. If there be any virtue in my example, emulate my faith. he who makes us just is also able and willing to give abundantly the faith we need and seek.

Your sermon and your epistle reached me much earlier than I had expected. I was anxious for your preaching word, and as I have prayed, new insights were given you and me. You see, my son, I have somewhat silently (if not secretly) wrestled with this problem of preaching "justification by faith alone" for many years. You know of my letters to those called to be saints at Galatia, Philippi, and Corinth. All these years, all our preaching and writing and teaching, and still we must proclaim to Jew and Gentile alike, the power of faith from God our Father to each of us, what I call *from faith to faith.*

This John Wesley that you spoke of and this Martin Luther, did my letters indeed, with much divine intervention, bode well for their salvation? Did these feeble writings of mine in any way cause them to believe or to become a part of the faithful? They too must have been called to be saints and to live not by the law but by love. I thank you for bringing their works to my mind. How I long to read and to know more of them. It does seem, my brother, that we are all called to a "Rome" . . . to an England . . . to your America.

But first, let me deal with the primary issue of your writing. You modern preachers are a puzzle to me. Have you all taken leave of your senses? What is this business of preaching to be profound, academic, and intellectual? By whose orders do you preach, and what is the priority and purpose of your preaching? If your desire is to prevail with academia, let me remind you that I too can boast of accomplishments. In Athens and in other regions of intellectual thought I have argued with the best of them.

But let me assure you that while we must not be simple preachers, the gospel remains a simple message: God loves us, Jesus died for us, and he will save us and bring us to be with him. This is the simplicity and the profundity of the gospel which must never be lost in our preaching. Never you mind being profound — preach Jesus! The only value which any preaching shall ever have is that it brings men to the acceptance of a faith which will endure today and tomorrow. Fundamental faith which issues from a fundamental gospel is that which ultimately will save the world.

Enough of my preaching. There are other matters of importance to you and to me. I make inquiry, Beecher, of your use of the word <u>saved</u>. How beautiful is this word, and particularly so in light of the manner by which you use it and the implications it carries for your people. Am I correct to believe that this concept comes from the word <u>salvation?</u>

If this be so, my salvation, my saving, readied me to preach the gospel of the One who saved me — who saved you, and who awaits the call for salvation of all who would hear the word and believe. In former days I wrote much of my own experience of conversion. Your letter and your sermon bring again to the fore my own thoughts on the matter. In these last days I seldom speak of it, for it is not my person who is of importance; rather it is the gospel I was given at my salvation which must take the preeminence.

Therefore, my son, I share with you that which has been revealed unto me regarding the faith of which you preach. Tell them, those who would be saved, that their belief in our Lord is not enough. Moreover, you must make them aware that faith is a given. There is no beginning; there is no end. Faith comes alone from God, my son, and is not under the authority of any man. Faith cannot be quantified; faith is.

I do not mean to be overcritical of your preaching. I am sure you seek to speak to your time and to the needs of the people whom you serve. God be praised for your faithfulness in this alone. Nevertheless, I am curious how any sermon on faith could be preached without a passing notice of Abraham. Abraham possessed what some are calling radical faith predicated on radical obedience. The sure lesson of Abraham, however, is that he knew only complete faith in our God and was faithful and obedient to his call to sacrifice Isaac, the treasured gift from God.

Where did Abraham's faith begin? Where did it end? Of a truth, we see no beginning; only a kind of faith which is acted out, a faith that is lived, a faith that has both wings and wheels. Does this not tell you, my brother, of the sustaining, holding, enduring power of faith?

There is no gainsaying that you chose a theme to preach which was difficult for you and for me. Nevertheless, it is a word that must be preached, a lesson that must be taught as long as there are those in the world and of the world who are not in salvation's plan; to wit, they have not been saved.

Finally, be of good courage, my son, be strong in the faith, and do not let questions which appear to be divorced and apart from the Spirit of Christ hinder your preaching of the gospel.

I must tell you, Beecher, your epistle written in faith is of the faith, and it was delivered to those called to be saints as a faithful apostle. Our Lord spoke each word with you — did you not sense his power and his presence? That too is from faith to faith; from his faith in us to our faith in him.

Do not forget that faith comes from those deep recesses of spirit which are within and cannot be applied from without. Faith will sustain you and those to whom you preach, even though you cannot define it or fathom it. Take this message to the near regions and far. It is your call to spread the gospel without fear or shame. Go in faith, with faith, for faith and he will be with you always. Peace be with you.

Your brother in faith,
Paul

4

RELIGION IN REVERSE

PROLOGUE

Washington, D.C.

Dear Paul:

Well, I've done it now!

I started to write this letter last night just as I was putting the final touches on the sermon, but I was so mentally exhausted from the effort that I just couldn't write another word. The strange thing is that I was disturbed by the implications of the word I was about to preach and equally as sure that it was a word that could not be denied—the gospel trumpet would be heard. So what I'm sending you now falls in the category of "sermons I wish I didn't have to preach." I told my congregation it was a sermon <u>most</u> preachers would <u>not</u> preach.

The interesting thing to me is that many of the problems of which you wrote in your letter to the Roman church are problems with which we are faced today. You never saw Washington, but some of the things you describe could fit here and most any American city. What we are faced with, Paul, is a social, moral, and ethical falling away from those values and virtues which have been the mainstay of civilized society. Washington is a city where $24 million <u>a day!</u> is spent on cocaine, a narcotic substance which many of our people use in order to get "high," a euphoric sense of well-being and happiness which inevitably leads to ruined lives and death. To look at our contemporary social order is to see a world that is going backward instead of forward, a world where everything is moving in reverse.

What disturbs me most about this sermon, Paul, is that I really wanted to express concern and understanding and compassion. I did not want to come across, in this sermon or in any other, as one who has no sensitivity to human suffering or to human failing. On the other hand, does there not come a time in all of preaching when the preacher must take a stand? Preachers cannot blink at sin either in themselves or in others.

We do come to the point, I think, when a word must be said about sin: that which separates man from man and that which alienates man from God. To see the same kind of self-destruction in our own social order as you described in the opening lines of your letter to the Romans and to say nothing would not be an act of compassion; it would be an act of condemnation. We simply cannot afford to mortgage the souls of men or women whose behavior does not bring life and may, in fact, be the highest heresy of idolatry.

Paul, I do not mean to preach to you. I share these thoughts simply so you will understand the great anxiety with which I approach the pulpit. All preachers must wrestle, I suspect, with the ethics of controversial preaching. Like you, I thank my God upon every remembrance of this band of Christians who have been committed to my care. Their love for me permits me to speak the word of truth in love, without fear or trepidation. A ruler in our time, Theodore Roosevelt, coined the phrase a "bully pulpit." He was referring to the power of the state, but the preacher's pulpit is a bully pulpit too.

By the way, were you ever really afraid when you said things that you knew would not be accepted or understood? (You can tell me! This is just between us preachers!) I find that being unashamed and being fearless are not the same commodity. It is in these moments of preaching that one tends to measure discretion and judgment. In any case, his Word must be preached and by his grace we so continue to do.

Your word in your last letter on the purpose and priority of preaching was welcomed. Thanks, I needed that!

Keep me always in your prayers. I remain

On dangerous ground,
Beecher

Sermon: RELIGION IN REVERSE
(A Sermon Most Preachers Won't Preach!)

Wherefore God also gave them up to uncleanness through the lusts of their own hearts, to dishonor their own bodies between themselves: Who changed the truth of God into a lie, and worshipped and served the creature more than the Creator, who is blessed forever. Amen (Romans 1:24–25).

Therefore thou art inexcusable, O man, whosoever thou art that judgest: for wherein thou judgest another, thou condemnest thyself; for thou that judgest doest the same things (Romans 2:1).

As I have been given to understand it, the goal of the biblical interpreter is to be able to see the truth of God even when such truth seems inaccessible and to be able to proclaim that truth even when the word of God seems, at best, mysterious and veiled. Unfortunately, as I have discovered it, even the finest interpreters among us, even the most incisive and insightful exegetes among us, more often than not, will find themselves standing with a sense of holy wonder, standing in reverential awe before the very word they are called upon to define.

One can see the word; one can read the word; but until one

is able to dissect and define and delineate the word that is in the Word, God's Word—God's authentic Word—is as yet unknown and unrevealed. And that is why, I should imagine, when the apostle Paul spoke of the mysterious and the majestic in God's Word, he described it as "seeing through a glass darkly."

The Unpopular Preacher

It ought to be acknowledged at the outset that this is a sermon that most preachers won't preach. It is not that this is a word not found in Scripture, for it is. It is not that this word is not a part of redeeming gospel, for it is. Nor is this a word that was never intended to be preached, for it was! Rather, what we have here is a sermon that may well cause concern before it is preached and will certainly cause conversation after it is preached. What we have here is a word that will put the preacher "on the line" with a controversial subject, and may even place in jeopardy the preacher's platform of popularity.

Admittedly, preachers ought not to entertain too many notions about popularity, and in any case, I pity the preacher whose primary purpose it is to be popular. You can't be popular and prophetic at the same time.

- Noah was not popular when he preached that sermon entitled "It's Gonna Rain!"
- Elijah was not popular when he told the 450 prophets of Baal, "If the Lord be God, follow him: but if Baal, then follow him."
- Isaiah was not popular when he told Hezekiah, "Set thine house in order: for thou shalt die, and not live."
- Nathan was not popular when he told David about his lecherous liaison with Bathsheba and said to him: "Thou art the man!"

But then, as I have been given to understand it, the preacher's job is not to be popular but to be faithful. The preacher's job is to declare the truth even when people don't want to hear the truth. The preacher's job is to preach the word—in season and out—even when people don't want to abide by the word. The goal of the biblical interpreter is to be able to see and to proclaim the truth of God even if one loses popularity in the process.

The Occasion

Now, simply as a means of refreshing your memory, you do recall that Paul sent this pastoral letter from his post in Corinth to the Christian community situated in Rome. It was Paul's desire, as you know, to visit Rome, but since his visit had been delayed and since his preaching of the gospel had carried him far afield, Paul wrote to the beloved of God, called to be saints, and assured them of his concern and of his prayers.

It is in this letter that Paul talks of the power of the gospel and of his commitment to its preaching. Paul was a Jew by birth, by training, and by rearing, and yet Paul declares that he is not ashamed of the gospel. Not only that, but this gospel which Paul preaches contains, as he said, the very righteousness of God that runs from faith to faith. It is faith at the time of one's beginning, and it remains faith until the time of one's end.

But now there is a shift. It is a shift both of theme and tone. It is a shift for which we were not prepared. It is a shift which could not have been predicted or foreseen. In verse 17, Paul speaks of the righteousness of God, but now here in verse 18, Paul shifts and speaks of the wrath of God. Paul speaks now of the *orge* of God, God's indignation, God's anger laced with pathos, God's irritation punctuated with passion. Paul is speaking now of the very anger of God.

To be sure, I realize that we may not want to deal with this issue, but Paul says that there are some things that just make God angry. There are some things that agitate and antagonize God. There are some things that get on God's last nerve!

- It makes God angry whenever he sees unrighteousness and ungodliness.
- It makes God angry whenever people use their unrighteousness to prevent the truth from being known.

- It makes God angry whenever people claim that they know him and yet, by their actions, do not honor him.
- It makes God angry whenever people who were created to worship God begin to worship the images created by man.

However, if you really want to know how angry God gets, if you really want to know what gets on God's last nerve, listen to this. Whenever God thinks about those who have angered him by their ungodliness and their unrighteousness, Paul says the result was that

> God . . . gave them up to uncleanness through the lusts of their own hearts, to dishonor their own bodies between themselves: who changed the truth of God into a lie, and worshipped and served the creature more than the creator.

Whenever men or women change the truth of God into a lie, whenever men or women take that which God has made by the hand of his own creative power and turn it inside out, whenever they take that which God has said is right and make it wrong, whenever men or women take the truth of God and turn it into a lie,

THAT IS RELIGION IN REVERSE, AND THAT MAKES GOD ANGRY!

Paul's Rome

Now, lest we get too quickly removed from the argument, it may be of value to share with you the nature of the world at the time Paul did his writing. William Barclay, in his exposition on the book of Romans, has suggested that the era in which these Romans lived was indeed an "Age of Shame." Some may want to suggest that Paul was no more than a hysterical moralist exaggerating his situation, but in point of fact, this was the age in which Rome experienced a degeneracy of morals almost without parallel in human history.

Virgil says that in this Rome, "Right and wrong [were] confounded."

It is a world where violence had run amok. Indeed, Tacitus

described the era as one "rich in disasters, gloomy with wars, rent with sedition, savage in its very hours of peace."

Propertius, the poet, wrote with appropriate pathos: "I see Rome, proud Rome perishing, the victim of her own prosperity."

The age to which Paul wrote was an age of moral suicide. Seneca said it was an age "stricken with the agitation of a soul no longer master of itself."

It was an age of unparalleled luxury. The Emperor Caligula had even sprinkled the floor of the circus arena with gold dust instead of saw dust.

It was an age of unparalleled immorality. History has it that Agrippina, the empress herself, wife of Claudius, was known to slip out of the palace at night and go down to the local house of prostitution simply for the sake of her own enjoyment. And even more than that, this was an age when fourteen of the first fifteen emperors of Rome were homosexuals.

Religion in Reverse

And so this is the world, this is the Rome to which Paul wrote. This is the Rome in which and to which Paul wanted to preach the gospel. This is the Rome to which Paul sent a word about the saving power of God. This is the Rome to which Paul dared to write about the righteousness of God. To this perverted social order Paul cried out: "The just shall live by faith!" But it is also the same Rome to which Paul was able to say fearlessly and without thought of personal peril or loss— they have "changed the truth of God into a lie." Paul told them that what Rome had was a kind of religion in reverse.

I want to share these thoughts about religion in reverse with you today because something is afoot on the religious horizon. What is occurring in the culture has had its impact on what is occurring in the church. These are days when it is hard to tell who's who and what's what. Not everyone who wears pants is a man and, in the spirit of equal opportunity, not everyone who wears a skirt is a woman.

Moreover, there is a sexual revolution abroad in the land.

A dread disease whose only end is death has struck fear into the hearts of men and women all over the land. We must be clear. AIDS is not simply a homosexual disease; it is a heterosexual disease too. But it has had its major impact within the "gay" or homosexual community. More than this, however, AIDS is not simply a physical virus. Where it has come as a result of moral indiscretion and poor judgment, it is a moral virus that is loose in the world. There is a sexual revolution in the land.

Consequently, they tell me that more people are coming to church in search of a life-mate, but the truth is that seemingly all of the available men are either already married, in jail, or have chosen an alternative lifestyle, which makes them unwilling and unsuitable candidates for marriage.

In the midst of all of this, the church must face honestly this problem of *religion in reverse*.

- Religion in reverse occurs when the things that should be are overridden by the things that should not be.
- Religion in reverse takes place when those who preach a message of behavior with no biblical root and no spiritual end are able to gain more converts than those who preach the gospel of Jesus Christ.
- Religion in reverse takes place when those who are in the church cannot speak a word to those outside of the church because their record of conduct disavows the Christ they claim to serve.
- Religion in reverse results when saints act like sinners.
- Religion in reverse exists when saints and swingers join up in church on Sunday morning and you can't tell which is which, when you can't tell the saints from the sinners or which swinger is swinging which saint.

That's religion in reverse.

It is not my intention or purpose to be offensive or argumentative or judgmental in this analysis of this text. However, I thought that perhaps we would do well to take a stroll down the corridors of this text to see if within this word of judgment there might be a word of redemption and salvation and hope as well.

At the outset, we ought to acknowledge that Paul is very explicit about what is going on in Rome, as a result of those who have given themselves over to the work of ungodliness and unrighteousness. Paul says:

- God gave them up unto vile affections.
- Women changed the natural use into that which is against nature.
- Men, leaving the natural use of the woman, burned in their lust toward one another.
- And finally, God gave them up to a reprobate mind or God gave them up to a "corrupted" mind, the kind of mind that everybody rejects and nobody wants.

Why was Paul so explicit? Why was Paul so graphic? Why was Paul so negative and so dogmatic and so descriptive of a situation with which those to whom he wrote were all too familiar? I hope Paul won't mind my wondering if he has a bit of the style of the Pharisee left in him. You see, I've been trying to get into the mind of Paul, and I believe that Paul wrote this as he did in part simply to say to those who were struggling to be Christian in an non-Christian world:

THIS IS WHAT SIN CAN DO!

Just in case you had not given much thought to the reality of sin, look at Rome. This is what sin can do!

Just in case you had not given much credence to the power of sin, look at Rome. This is what sin can do.

Just in case you thought that sin had no contemporary relevance or lasting consequence, perhaps you ought to look at Rome. This is what sin can do.

Just in case you thought that all you had were one or two insignificant vices that don't really matter that much, maybe you ought to look at Rome. This is what sin can do.

There is no question but that there is value here as we take a look at this uncomfortable text. A strange leading of the Spirit of Christ leads me to preach this sermon that most preachers won't preach because I, for one, am convinced that the church cannot afford to be silent on the subject of sin. The church cannot blink its eyes at that sin which willfully goes against the way God meant things to be.

I know that *sin* is an old-fashioned notion. We live in a modern age that exalts personal expression and worships at the altar of independence, but somebody ought to say, "Look what sin can do!"

I know we live in a modern age that is highly protective of individual rights and the pursuit of personal pleasure and preference, but maybe somebody ought to say, "Look what sin can do!"

I know we live in a modern age that has let down the barriers of puritanical moralisms in preference to a philosophy of life that simply says: "If it feels good, go for it," but, before it's too late, I thought somebody really ought to be bold enough in the Lord to say: "Look what sin can do!"

- Sin caused Solomon to say that "righteousness exalts a nation but sin is a reproach to any people."
- Sin: Isaiah said that sin was just like crimson and red like scarlet.
- Sin: Paul said it was a universal predicament because "all have sinned and fallen short of the glory of God."
- Sin caused David to declare: "I was shapen in iniquity and in sin did my mother conceive me."
- Sin caused David to confess: "I acknowledge my transgressions and my sin is ever before me."

And, every once in a while, if you know the power of sin, if you know the reality of sin, if you know what sin can do, you need to say:

> Create in me a clean heart, O God;
> and renew a right spirit within me. . . .
>
> Purge me with hyssop, and I shall be clean:
> wash me, and I shall be whiter than snow. . . .
>
> Restore unto me the joy of thy salvation;
> and uphold me with thy free spirit.
>
> (Psalm 51:10, 7, 12)

The Creation Narrative

But I hear somebody saying, "Brother Preacher, what sin are you talking about?" Well, in the words of A. Louis Patterson: "I'm glad you asked that question!"

If you look into the book of Genesis, you will discover that God created man. God created man and woman. Not only did he create them, he talked with them. God and man conversed with each other. God knew man and man knew God. But somewhere in that same Genesis story, man rejected God. Man knew the truth about God. He knew who God was and where God was and what God was doing. Everything man needed to know about God, man knew.

But man, on his own and by the exercise of his free will, decided that he did not want the God-factor in his life. Man rebelled. Man fell out with God. Man in the garden *then* wanted to do what he wanted to do. Man in the garden *now* wants to do what he wants to do. Man wanted to live by his own rules and by his own authority. Man wanted to use God's garden, but he did not want to abide by God's rules. Man wanted to eat the fruit of God's garden and drink from the fountain in God's garden but did not want to be obedient to the God who provided the garden.

And that's why man, the tenant, became man, the thinker, because he thought he could out-think the God who gave him the mind to think in the first place. That's why man, the sharecropper, became man, the scientist, because he thought he understood creation better than the Creator. That's why man, the lessee, became man, the philosopher, because he believed he had more wisdom than the Source of wisdom.

Because man and God were not on the same wavelength, man discovered that he was without a God. And because man is at base a religious being, (what the Latins call "homo religioso") man decided that he had to worship something, even if he had to worship himself.

Now, lest you suspect that I am not "in the Word," when you look at Genesis 3:5 you will discover that the serpent, Satan, told Adam and Eve that they didn't need to worry about God because, just as soon as they ate of the tree, "ye shall be as gods." The point is, that if man is his own god, he can do whatever he pleases. If man is his own god, he can fulfill all his desires. If man is his own god, then the creature has become more important than the Creator. If man is his own god, then man takes God's place, and God takes man's place, and that's religion in reverse.

Consequently, when you read Paul's letter to the Romans and compare it with what is going on in America today—men acting like women and women acting like men . . .

- The problem is not human sexuality.
- The problem is not heredity or environment.
- The problem is not personal or chemical or biological.
- The problem is not the pastor putting his own value system on the congregation.
- The problem is not with the world or the church trying to determine what is normative or natural or expected.
- The problem is not that any one is attempting to take away the right of choice or preference or individuality.

The problem is *idolatry!*

- Anytime man worships anything other than God, that's idolatry.
- Anytime man thinks that what man wants is more important than what God wants, that's idolatry.
- Anytime man moves from self-indulgence to self-deification, it's not very far from immorality to idolatry.
- And every once in a while, even a preacher who loses popularity has to tell men and women that God said: "Thou shalt have no other gods before me!"

Now, I want to say a word to those who think I'm not preaching to them. You see, Paul gives a list of folk who fall into like categories as those who have a sexual lifestyle different from yours. This list includes the unrighteous, fornicators, the wicked, the covetous, those who are malicious, those full of envy, murderers, debaters (those looking for prestige and prominence), the deceitful, the devious and the underhanded, whisperers and slanderers (those who tell everything they know), the haters of God, the despiteful and the proud, those who hate others simply for the sake of hurting them, the arrogant, those who have contempt for everyone except themselves, the boasters, those who pretend they have what they have not, those without natural affection, who don't love anything or anybody, the implacable and the unmerciful.

Paul says this includes you. This includes you because you didn't read Romans 2:1.

> Therefore thou art inexcusable, O man, whosoever thou art that judgest: for wherein thou judgest another, thou condemnest thyself; for thou that judgest doest the same things.

Paul is not just talking about one sin, he's talking about Sin. Sin is asexual. I don't care whether its homosexual sin or heterosexual sin. Sin is just sin. And the preacher's job is to tell men like the slaves of old:

> You better mind, my brother,
> How you walk on the cross;
> Your foot might slip
> And your soul be lost.

The preacher's job is to say, like Paul, "The wages of sin is death; but the gift of God is eternal life."

I began by telling you that this is a sermon that most preachers won't preach. But this may be the only sermon that preachers ought to preach.

In the midst of all of this sin and shame, in the midst of all of this degradation and perversion, Paul said, "I am ready to preach the gospel to you that are at Rome also." Not only that, but Paul said, "I am not ashamed of the gospel of Christ: for it is the power of God unto salvation to everyone that believeth." And, I preach this gospel today because I believe this gospel has the power to change people's lives. If I did not believe that, I would close my Bible and take off my robes.

You see, I don't care what you're into; God has the power to get you out of it. There is no habit that you are bound to keep. God has the power to get you out of it. There is no sin that you just must commit. God has the power to get you out of it. I don't care who or what you are, God can deliver you.

- If you'll let him, he will deliver. He will deliver heterosexuals, homosexuals, lesbians, transvestites, transsexuals, bisexuals, adulterers, pimps, and prostitutes.

▪ If you'll let him, he'll make your life complete; he'll give you joy complete. If you let him, you'll go down from this place singing in your soul:

What a wonderful change in my life has been wrought
Since Jesus came into my heart!
I have light in my soul for which long I had sought
Since Jesus came into my heart!

EPILOGUE

Ephesus

Beecher, my son and my brother in the faith:

"Religion in Reverse." Well, you really took on a serious subject this time, didn't you? I am proud of you and your God-given courage to preach the truth as you see it. I am proud of your willingness to speak this word, knowing that others will not see it as you see it. There is power in preaching, my son — preach the Word. This is our calling and our claim.

I am anxious to know how this message was received by your saints. Did anyone accept Christ? Was anyone converted in response to this gospel? No one wants to hear about God's wrath or God's anger, especially when it hits so close to home.

Sin is an awesome word, my son, and if sin is religion in reverse, then salvation is that which stops the reversal and makes conversion, a turning about, possible through Christ.

I would not make light here of your apostolic gifts, Beecher. I know from past and present experience that these words of mine are the hardest you will ever seek to preach through. But you must preach. Put on your armor, prepare for spiritual warfare, and stand fast in the Lord. Without question you will have your night of defeat and death. Gethsemane is always with us. Do not forget that I was stoned; my life was threatened more than once; I was adrift at sea for days without end. But we won, Beecher. We won.

If there be any consolation, perhaps you can gain strength from my example that you can preach an uncompromising gospel. But you must never shrink from the high price which must be paid for the privilege of preaching. The price itself is the down payment on even more substantial power for the days which are to come.

You asked for my analysis. Well, this is it. There was a sincere attempt to be even-handed here. While you told your hearers that God does not tolerate that which perverts and distorts the purposes of his creative impulse and energy, while you told them that God would not tolerate their worship of themselves, and while you warned them not to judge others while they are involved in other counter-productive behavior, that even those who thought that they had escaped would suffer a similar condemnation — while you did all this, I sensed a kind of question mark that hovered over the entire presentation.

My son, there is no easy way to preach on the sin issue. He who would be used of God must decide to speak or to remain silent. There can be no middle of the road, nor should there be, for we must direct men not to the broad way, which all have found, but to the narrow way which very few have discovered.

Beecher, I must be completely candid with you. Despite your protestations to the contrary, I sense that you really _are_ concerned about your popularity among your people. This does not come as a result of anything you have said; it is rather a response to what I am feeling. No one told either of us on our conversion roads that all the people would hear us and love us. In fact, the reverse is true. Whenever the people love you and accept you and never reject you, you may be certain that they have listened to you, but they have not heard you. That is what it means to be a preacher.

To preach this word was painful for you, and I assure you that to write this word is painful for me. Yet, as you are aware, sin is still sin, right is right, and in the eyes of God there can be no compromise with evil. At the same time, we are gospel preachers, and that causes us, as we preach a word of judgment, also to bring a word of Good News! It is good news to know that the lost can be found, the rejected can be accepted, and those who are far off can and will find deliverance.

Above all, Beecher, remember that I am your shoulder to lean on and the impartial sounding board you need for your times of questions and doubt. Seeing your approach to this subject, I wonder: If I had taken a similar path, what would the result have been when this letter was first delivered to the saints at Rome? If the goal of the gospel is to penetrate the human heart, then your sermon must surely have done so.

Continue instant in the preaching of the gospel of Jesus Christ. Have you found it to be the case that just when you think your preaching has come to nothing, God gives to it his greatest benediction? Have you ever come to the end of your preaching, knowing that it was a feeble, ineffective, sorry example of the exercise of the craft, and just as you were about to take your seat in defeat, people have come from everywhere to accept the Christ whom you have proclaimed? That, my son, is God's way of reminding us that this preaching business is his and not ours. At best we are leaky vessels through whom his word is poured. How strange it is that when we believe we have failed, he is able to use us to his glory. And in that act itself our calling is justified and fulfilled.

Beecher, we must simply remain available to be the vessels he can use, even though we do not understand the process. Through it all God is praised.

I thank my God for you always in my prayers that you will be able, having done all, to stand! Grace, mercy, and peace from God the Father, God the Son, and God the Holy Spirit. Amen.

Your brother in the battle,
Paul

5

I'VE GOT A SECRET

PROLOGUE

Washington, D.C.

Dear Paul:

I'm hurting. Every preacher in this region is hurting. If I don't talk with you—if I don't talk with someone—I feel I'm going to lose it (an expression we have for losing one's hold on sanity).

Paul, do you remember that scandal that rocked the church at Corinth? The one involving incest? Well we have had a scandal here that has rocked the church. Some of our most vocal and visible preachers have been caught in sexual sins, and their behavior has become the focus of the evening news on national television.

What bothers me, my brother, is not the scandal itself but the fact that it has exposed the belief in our country that preachers should be above human failure. There is an insistence on perfection among preachers which simply is not the case. Preachers are weak, fearful, completely human creatures. We seek to be faithful to the Word we preach (most of us, at least). But there are many times when we need to be preached to, to be reminded of our sinful nature and our potential for fall. Now people are gleefully exposing every sin and shortcoming they can find in a preacher's life. Now that they have exposed a few, how long can it be before they come after the rest of us?

Do not mistake my meaning, Paul. I am not trying to excuse unethical or immoral conduct. What I am questioning is whether we preachers have preached so much about sin that we have failed to say enough about grace? I am aggravated and disturbed, not because of what has been revealed, but because of the damage which may have been done to the cause of Christ. For many the church was already irrelevant, but if now it is seen as unredemptive even for its most ardent spokespersons, what shall we say—what shall we do?

Let's be honest, Paul, we all have secrets. But tell me, what is the end result when all the lights are turned on, when all the secrets are seen, when the real is revealed and when the whispers are shouted from the rooftops? I know I have secrets. And I'll bet you had some secrets too. You said a lot in your letters, Paul, yet I can't help but imagine there were some unfinished sentences and some incomplete thoughts which never got circulated and which never came to print.

I've got to hurry now because I want to get this letter and my latest sermon off to you, so I can get your response before I preach this sermon on secrets. Even preaching on this subject is scary because I don't want people to think that I am titillating or teasing them. This is a serious matter, and I want them to know that all judgment must be tempered with justice, to know that the only antidote for sin is grace.

I wish I had time to write more, but the latest issue of the National Misinformer is on the stands, and I don't want to miss my copy.

Hope to hear from you soon.

Grace and peace,
Beecher

Sermon: I'VE GOT A SECRET

(For not the hearers of the law are just before God, but the doers of the law shall be justified. For when the Gentiles, which have not the law, do by nature the things contained in the law, these, having not the law, are a law unto themselves: Which shew the work of the law written in their hearts, their conscience also bearing witness, and their thoughts the mean while accusing or else excusing one another;) In the day when *God shall judge the secrets of men by Jesus Christ* according to my gospel (Romans 2:13–16).

By any comparison the apostle Paul was a craftsman of the written word. As a missionary, the legacy of churches founded throughout the whole of Asia Minor stood as testimony to his organizational skill and his leadership ability. As a preacher Paul never stood in any prestigious pulpit, nor would he have had the opportunity to climb the preaching stair of any cathedral in this time. As a man of charisma and charm it is doubtful that his would have been an impressive presence. For as you know, he did tend to walk with a limp due to some unfortunate physical ailment which he described as "a thorn in the flesh" and the "agent of Satan."

And yet, for all that Paul was and for all that Paul was not, there is no question in my mind but that by any comparison the apostle Paul was a craftsman of the written word.

Paul's letter to the church at Rome which was transported on the wings of a Corinthian postage stamp is, no doubt, the finest example we have of Paul's ability as a communicator of the gospel of Jesus Christ. You do recall, of course that Paul would have gained his writing skills while matriculating in the Hebrew schools at Jerusalem and while a student at the feet of Gamaliel. Paul was by no means an itinerant, run-of-the-mill, jack-leg preacher. Quite to the contrary, Paul was a rabbi of rabbis, a scholar's scholar, and a preacher's preacher. Paul's every word reflects the cultural climate of his rearing and the unmistakable birthright of his breeding. But above all else, Paul's writing is reflective of the fact that somewhere in this life he did have an intimate encounter with the Eternal.

How else does one account for the genius in his writing? How else does one account for this ancient-day wordsmith who used poetry in his prose and wrote prose as though it were poetry?

Who else but Paul could write a word of judgment on the misuse of spiritual gifts and at the same time a self-analysis on the quality of his own preaching? Said Paul:

> Though I speak with the tongues of men and of angels and have not love I am become as sounding brass, or a tinkling cymbal.

Who else but Paul could write a word that would summon troops to battle and yet write that word in step with the music in his soul? Said Paul:

> If the trumpet give an uncertain sound, who shall prepare himself to the battle?

Who else but Paul could write with such sensitivity to the human predicament that even when he speaks of the sunshine and the shadows in his own life, every word has the authentic ring of one who has borne the burden in the heat of the day? Said Paul:

> I have learned, in whatsoever state I am, therewith to be content. I know both how to be abased, and I know how to abound: every where and in all things I am instructed both to be full and to be hungry, both to abound and to suffer need. I can do all things through Christ which strengtheneth me.

Who else but Paul could write whether in the midst of a storm-tossed sea or in the loneliness of a cold and dark prison cell?

Who else but Paul could write with such vividness of expression that we can see him thrown from his beast somewhere on the Damascus Road?

And who can write with such a flare for descriptive phraseology that we can feel every rock and jolt of that earthquake down in Philippi when Silas sang and Paul prayed?

All of this forms the basis for my insistence that by any

standard of comparison, the apostle Paul was a craftsman of the written word.

Now, just in case you have some question regarding the significance and the relevance of Paul's ability as a writer, let me remind you that the strength of Paul's work as a missionary preacher was not achieved because of his ecclesiastical status in the largest church in town. In case you had forgotten, Paul was never called to be the rabbi down at the synagogue in Jerusalem. The value of Paul's ministry cannot be measured by the length of the flowing rabbinical robes which might well have draped about his shoulders in some evangelistic crusade. Perhaps the significance of Paul's writings has not dawned upon you, but I thought you ought to be reminded that the theology of the New Testament church received its frame and focus primarily because of the writing of an itinerant preacher from Tarsus whose given name was Saul, but whom the Lord renamed Paul.

I have raised the issue of Paul's incomparable writing style because the student of Pauline thought will be interested not only in what Paul says, but how Paul says it. Here in the second chapter of Paul's letter to the Roman church, Paul has dealt at length with the uncomfortable matter of sin and judgment. Paul has barely moved into the substance of his epistle when he gives a rather lengthy listing of those whose sins and shortcomings are on equal par with those who, as Paul would have it, God had given up "to a reprobate mind to do those things which are not convenient."

But now, to be fair to Paul, and to be sure that you understand the purpose of what may appear to have been an unjustified judgmental diatribe by a preacher whose credentials may well be questioned in some quarters, Paul raises these issues in the first and second chapters not as a means of pointing out the faults of one group over another, but to tell them that fundamentally there is no difference in sin. Because we are "all God's children," there is no such thing as Jewish sin or Gentile sin, male sin or female sin, homosexual sin or heterosexual sin. . . . Paul says, sin is sin and "God is no respecter of persons."

However, in the midst of his writing, Paul places a parenthesis. I was taken by this assertion of a parenthesis, clearly an exception and not the norm in the writing of this first-century apostle.

- A parenthesis is a sentence within a sentence, a thought within a thought, a necessary digression in the mind of the author.
- A parenthesis is used grammatically to indicate a break in the thought of the writer with a matter which demands the immediate concern of the reader.
- A parenthetical thought is an unavoidable interruption along the path of a logical journey with an idea or a concept that will not wait another moment for expression.
- A parenthesis sets a new idea apart from the whole and says "take note, pay attention, you better listen because what I have to say is important to you and to those who may chance to read it."

At the risk of being repetitive, you must understand that when Paul wrote these words he wrote them as a Jewish rabbi to a community dominated by those who were Jews by birth and now found themselves in close contact with Gentiles. Here then were Jews who, as a result of their conversion experience, had claimed Christ in their lives but at the same time laid claim to the privileges of their Jewishness. After all, Jews did not deal with Gentiles.

- Jews were saved. Gentiles were not.
- Jews were the chosen people, the recipients of the law. Gentiles were not.
- Jews were the direct descendants of Abraham. Gentiles were not.
- Jews were going to heaven. Gentiles were going to hell.

As a result of this rather narrow and spiritually elitist thought pattern among the Jews, Paul's objective was quite simple and pure. Jews who knew the law would be judged by the law. Gentiles who did not know the law would be judged as ones who did not know the law, even though it concerned Paul that very often Gentiles behaved as though they knew the law, and Jews behaved as though they had never heard the law. Nevertheless, whether one knew the law or not, Paul suggested that both Jews and Gentiles knew the difference between right and wrong and, therefore, neither could expect exemption from the judgment of God who, as Paul said, "will render to every man according to his deeds."

That is the reason for Paul's parenthesis. Says Paul, "While I'm dealing with this issue of the nature of sin, while I'm trying to define sin and how God deals with sin, maybe I'd better tell you a few things *parenthetically*. Maybe it might be advantageous to all parties concerned if I could shed some light on the sin issue *parenthetically*. Maybe it might be helpful if I could sort of focus my spiritual spotlight on some important factors in the sin circumstance. And so the first thing that I need to tell you is that *those who have a right relationship with God are not those who merely walk around carrying the Bible and reading the Bible, but those who do what the Bible says*. The mark of authentic religion is not whether you are hand-clappin', foot-pattin', Bible-totin', and Scripture quotin', but whether you put into practice what it is that you are reading.

- It's just a parenthesis, but Mr. and Mrs. Every-Sunday-Churchgoer ought to know that it's not what you do when you come in *here*, but what you do when you go back out *there* that counts.
- It's just a parenthesis, but Mrs. Long-Robe-Choir-Member ought to be advised that singing won't save you and solos won't redeem you if you don't live the life you sing about in your songs.
- It's just a parenthesis, but the Reverend Dr. Long-Winded-Preacher needs to be reminded that real preaching has no power until you practice what you preach.

And that is essentially what Paul meant to say when he added this parenthetical comment: "For not the hearers of the law are just before God, but the doers of the law shall be justified."

And yet, having said all of this, Paul is not satisfied. The substance of the sermon has been preached. Nevertheless, beyond his parenthesis, the preacher in Paul makes him press his claim further still. After a sermon on sin and judgment for Gentiles and Jews—no compromise, no exceptions, no alternatives—church is out! It's all over. Nothing else is needed but the benediction. But if you read verse 13 with verse 16, you'll see that Paul says I thought you ought to know, just to add some specific information, that this judgment will take place *"in the day when God shall judge the secrets of men by Jesus Christ."*

Now, this comment by Paul that God shall judge the secrets of men is indeed an awesome word. It is one thing to be held accountable for those failings which everyone can see. It is one thing to be called to account for those indiscretions which are transparent and which can be easily seen by those with whom we come into contact. It is one thing to confess and acknowledge and own up to sin and, as it were, to throw ourselves on the mercy of the court. But when it comes to *secrets*, that's another matter.

Have you given thought to this matter? How would you fare if your secrets were revealed? It's a terrible thing when the secret you thought was your secret, that *nobody* knew, is on your indictment sheet. It's an awesome, frightening thought to realize that one day the real person will be revealed, the hidden will come to light, and that which is "whispered in secret" will be shouted from the housetops.

Because this matter of secrets is so explosive and so volatile and because the revelation of secrets and the exposure of secrets can be so dangerous and destructive, I've been looking again at Paul's word here about God's judgment of the secrets of men. I realize that I stand in the midst of a time and in the midst of a society that takes a kind of satanic and demonic pleasure in scandalizing names and ruining reputations. It is quite clear to all concerned that every person comes to the point in his or her life when the news must be declared: *"I've got a secret!"*

I assure you that everybody has a secret. Whatever you do, do not look to your left, do not look to your right; simply take my word for it that everybody has a secret. Husbands have secrets they have not told their wives. Wives have secrets they have not told their husbands. The young and the old, the rich and the poor, Republicans and Democrats, conservatives and liberals . . . *and God knows preachers have secrets* . . . we all have secrets.

On the other hand, I wanted to tell you that not only does everybody have a secret, but if *you* have a secret, somebody wants to know your secret. You may not realize it, but all of your friends and surely all of your enemies would stand in line if they could hear your secret. Because we live in an age which has been characterized by an information explosion, secrets are a thing of the past. Nobody can keep a secret because there are too many folk who make it their business to discover your secret.

We live in an age that specializes in discovering other people's secrets. We live in a technologically sophisticated age that specializes in covert operations and undercover surveillance, bugging buildings and tapping phones, and even letting the air out of tires just to trap you and your secret. Secrets are a thing of the past, I tell you. This is the reason for those standing in line at the grocery store who cannot get past the checkout counter without buying the *Globe* and the *Star*. And we buy the *National Enquirer* because we're not satisfied with the local news. We want the latest and the juiciest gossip from all over the country.

The successful patterns of exposure in the realm of the political and the religious make it patently clear that no one can keep a secret. Even the shows we watch on television are designed to tell us who's keeping a secret from whom.

- Everybody wants to know what secret mischief Alexis is up to as she schemes to destroy Blake and Crystal on *Dynasty*.
- Everybody wants to know what secret schemes will show up in the suburbs with Val and Gary and Mack and Karen on *Knots Landing*.
- Everybody is listening for the rumor mill down near the vineyards where Richard and Maggie and Angela and Lance and Melissa try to keep secrets from each other on *Falcon Crest*.

- And even though they all live in the same house, it's a sure thing that Bobby can't keep any secrets from Lisa and J.R. can't keep any secrets from Sue Ellen on *Dallas*.

Secrets. You can't keep any secrets. People have learned how to discover even your secret secrets. And they have discovered that they don't have to go to *Another World* to look in on the *Days of Our Lives*. *All My Children*, even those who are *Bold and Beautiful* know that one day all secrets of the *Lives of the Rich and Famous* will be exposed just as sure *As the World Turns*. And if you want to know why the *Young and the Restless* are on the way to *General Hospital* it's because Cricket confronted Jessica, and Jill wanted Rex to propose, but he had already asked Kay, and Brad and Traci want to have a baby, while Leanna is busy telling lies to Ashley. And that's why I thought I ought to tell you about this secret business, since you only have *One Life to Live* and you need a *Guiding Light*, perhaps you'd like to know today that all of this other stuff doesn't really count, because if you want to know the truth, I've got a secret!

Lest you miss the point of all of this: We can become so enamored with the secrets of others that we fail to give attention to the secrets of our own lives and to our own relationship to God.

Paul says that it will be in that day that God shall judge the secrets of men. Well, tell us preacher, what are the secrets of men and what lessons are to be learned about the secrets of men? Tell us preacher, what can I do about my secrets, and what can I do about my secret secrets?

As a consequence of your questions, I thought it might be helpful if I discussed this matter with David. I looked for David.

- I looked for him out where the battle was going on with the Philistines.
- I looked for him down by the well at Bethlehem.
- I looked for him in his usual pasture, by his usual still waters, tending his flock of sheep.
- I looked for him somewhere playing his harp.
- I looked for him somewhere making up architectural plans for a temple he would never build.

I looked everywhere I could, but when I finally found him, when I finally caught up with David, I found him in a prayer meeting. I heard David praying Psalm 90:

> Lord, thou hast been our dwelling place in all generations. Before the mountains were brought forth, or ever thou hadst formed the earth and the world.

Whenever there are secrets in your life, that's the time to say:

> Father, I stretch my hands to thee, no other help I know.

When your sins are showing, that's the time to say:

> It's me, it's me, O Lord, standing in the need of prayer.

I heard David praying:

> Thou hast set our iniquities before thee, our secret sins in the light of thy countenance.

I'm not sure what the secrets of men are, but if, as David suggests, you've got some secret sins . . . if you've got some undercover sins, some presumptuous sins, some confidential sins, some behind-the-scenes sins, some sins on the "Q.T." . . . David says that if you've got some secret sins, your sins are standing in the light of his countenance. I don't have any sophisticated theology for it, but Granddaddy used to say:

> He sees everything you do, he hears every word you say.

Even more so, the old saying is still true: "You can run, but you can't hide."

I have discovered, as a result of this inquiry, that if my sin is standing in the "light of his countenance," I ought to be so busy trying to deal with my sins that I wouldn't have time to try to keep up with the sins of others.

Let me see if I can make this plain. As long as you've got some secrets, I wouldn't bother trying to expose another's secrets. You see it's a terrible thing when you try to dig a ditch for somebody else. When you try to dig a ditch for somebody else, you might as well dig it for two, because you're going to be in the ditch as well. Go further and ask Haman. It's dangerous to build a gallows for Mordecai. It could be you who will wind up swinging at the end of the rope you planned for another. No need in trying to find out what's going on in your neighbor's house; you need to deal first with what's going on in your house. Jesus said it doesn't make sense to get all bent out of shape about that speck in your brother's eye when you haven't gotten that two-by-four out of your own. Life's lessons are fairly fundamental: as long as you live in a glass house, don't you throw bricks at anyone else.

"All have sinned and fallen short of the glory of God." If I were you I wouldn't find my joy in another person's faults and failures. Isaiah said, "All we like sheep have gone astray." But just in case you've forgotten, I wanted to tell you: I've got a secret!

Since Paul was the one who brought this matter of secrets up in the first place, I wonder what Paul's secret is? I mean, since Paul is so confident that God will judge the secrets of men, and since Paul insists that "all have sinned," and since Paul is made of mortal flesh, and since Paul's feet are also made of clay, I'd just like to know what is Paul's secret?

I've been rumbling around in Paul's closet and I've seen that a long time ago this same Paul, when his name was still Saul, participated in a public demonstration of violence when he held the coats for men who stoned deacon Stephen to death.

This same Paul has a criminal record because I see here that he's been in jail more times than he can remember.

Not only that, but it has been rumored that this same Paul has some psychological problems. I heard Paul say: "For that which I do I allow not. For what I would, that do I not; but what I hate, that do I. . . . For the good that I would I do not: but the evil which I would not, that I do." There is even some suggestion (2 Corinthians 5:13) that Paul may be "beside" himself; there is even a question about his sobriety.

I have discovered that Paul had a little problem with his own self-esteem. Didn't you hear Paul say: "Oh, wretched man that I am! Who shall deliver me from the body of this death?"

Because Paul raised the secret issue, I would like to know what Paul's secret may be.

I have discovered that Paul knows how to deal with secrets. Paul deals with secrets by admitting them. I hear Paul saying:

- It is true, I've been beaten with rods.
- It is true, I've been stoned nearly to the point of death.
- It is true, I've been shipwrecked on a wild and stormy sea.
- It is true, I've been in court with no lawyer to plead my case.
- It is true, I've been in prison without my books or my coat.
- It is true, that Demas forsook me and Alexander the coppersmith did me great harm.

But if you really want to know my secret, the thing that helped me make it was, . . .

- When it stormed on the sea, God sent an angel.
- When I was in jail in Philippi, God sent an earthquake.
- When I was trapped in Thessalonica, God sent a basket to let me down on the other side.
- When I was stoned, God saved me.
- When I stood before Agrippa and Felix, God stood by my side.
- When I was down on the Damascus Road, God picked me up and turned me around.

When I became a cripple and could not walk up straight, I asked the Lord three times to remove the thorn [this thorn so closely guarded from disclosure] from my flesh, but he gave me another secret instead. This is the secret: "My grace is sufficient for thee: for my strength is made perfect in weakness."

I still hear somebody saying, "Brother Preacher, you told us you had a secret. And we've been waiting a long time, but we want to know what *your* secret is. It's all right to know about David's secret sins. It's interesting to learn about Paul's secret. But would you tell us, Brother Preacher, what is your secret?"

Well, I don't mind telling you my secret:

- I am a sinner, but I'm saved by grace!
- I'm up sometime, and I'm down sometime.
- I'm right sometime, and I'm wrong sometime.

There have been times when I should have walked right when I wound up walking left.

There have been times when I've said things that I should not have said and done things that I should not have done. But when I think about where I've been and how far the Lord has brought me, I think I ought to tell you the secret.

You see I've got this secret place. Every time I get a chance I go to my secret place. And I've discovered that when I dwell in my secret place, I can abide under the shadow of the Almighty. I've got a secret place. And I have discovered that it's best for me to go there all by myself. In fact, . . .

> I come to the garden alone
> While the dew is still on the roses.
> And the voice I hear falling on my ear
> The Son of God discloses.
> And he walks with me
> And he talks with me
> And he tells me I am his own.
> And the joy we share as we tarry there
> None other has ever known.

Do you hear me? I've got a *secret* place, and in my *secret* place I've got a *secret* weapon. You see, my *secret* weapon is this:

> I have a friend who I can tell all my troubles to.
> When I am burdened and I don't know what to do,
> I go to Jesus in secret prayer and
> I can leave all my burdens there.
> I know the Lord will make a way,
> Yes, he will!

I've got a secret place, and in my secret place I've got a secret weapon. But I thought you ought to know that my secret is not a secret. In fact, . . .

It is no secret what God can do.
What he's done for others
He'll do for you!
With arms wide open, he'll pardon you.
It is no secret what God can do.

No matter who you are, or what you are, or what you have become, no matter what your secret or your secret secret, it is no secret that he will pardon you, it is no secret that he will look beyond your fault and see your need. On that you can rely.

EPILOGUE

Tarsus

Beecher, my brother:

Such a beautiful day in Tarsus, and my friend delivered your letter and your sermon to me very early in the afternoon. I sensed the urgency of your tone, and therefore I put everything aside so that I would be able to read it all before the sun set. Let me put you at ease, my son. I share your pain as well as your joy.

On a personal note, I hope that you will be able to read my writing. As you know, I have adjusted my writing style to a much larger print, and I am using a broader stylus. With the passing of every day I sense more and more that my eyesight is growing weaker and, therefore, I must compensate with these large letters.

I must confess that I became so involved in your letter and in your sermon that I really wished I had been able to deliver my response by hand. How often the spoken word is heard "louder" than a written word. I long for the opportunity to pray and to preach and to worship with you and with the Christians at Washington and Metropolitan, particularly so that you are now dealing with these internal matters of heart and mind and spirit.

As much as I would want to come to Washington, I am confident that you have had some secret desire to come to Rome. I don't know if Rome is ready for you just yet, Beecher. Rome would have made a prestigious pulpit, wouldn't it? I have often wondered — secretly — if this is why I really wanted to go there so desperately. I say "secretly," Beecher, because I have yet to feel as comfortable as you seem to be in talking about my humanity with the saints.

When I was a practicing Pharisee — a true scholar of the law — I knew whereof I spoke. Beecher, I knew each section, chapter, precedent, and tort of the law. But the law lacked life — a saving substance; it offered no salvation and was apart from the life in Jesus Christ. I shudder and tremble when I remember those wasted, precious years. Those who specialize in the law are those who delight in the transgressions of others, and therefore they spend great time and gain great delight in revealing the secrets of others.

Perhaps, Beecher, there are some vital lessons to be learned as a result of the failures of your brothers in the ministry. As God is my witness, we must not forget that there is a danger in claiming to be something that we are not. If we tell people that we live without sin or above sin, or that we are not touched by sin, we will be held accountable to that claim. In every way I thank my God that I am ever aware of the wretched man that I am.

This very nasty business which has scandalized the church in your region also teaches that as long as we are free moral agents, we must also be responsible moral agents. We are held accountable first to God and, second, to those we serve and certainly to ourselves. If there be any virtue in what I have written, Beecher, it may well be that I have made you see clearly that the wages of sin is death — more spiritual than physical, more ethical than social — even for preachers.

I confess I was somewhat amused by your rather clumsy attempt to reveal my secret. Preachers have been doing that for generations now. Most of that I made no attempt to keep a secret; you know how people talk about small things and make them large. Most of those "secrets" to which you refer are really my badges of honor; they are the marks in my body. All I have said is sufficient — I have a thorn in my flesh, and it is not necessary that I reveal it or discuss it with anyone other than the One who gave it me.

It tends to make me limp, this thorn; as a result I am something of a cripple. Most of us are cripples, if not physically then spiritually. Often those closest to us cannot see our crutches. Why don't we simply agree, Beecher, that I will not tamper with your secrets if you will not tamper with mine. The day when the secrets of all hearts shall be revealed will come soon enough.

You are correct, my brother, my encounter on that roadside university just outside of Damascus, in most circles, does not qualify me to preach our Lord's gospel. Thank God for not being a member of that "circle!" He called me and he called you; he equipped me and he did likewise you. Whenever I have failed a test, he has allowed me to try again. I thank my God that all errors are not fatal and that all mistakes are not eternal. We serve a God of a second chance. This is a word which must be preached and practiced in all the churches among all the saints.

This final, personal, note is necessary. I am convinced that you (or any preacher) cannot preach as you are so called to do without the validation of the Holy Spirit of God, who has laid his hands on you. Despite our secrets, we have all thought, said, and done things for which we are not proud. The glory of the gospel is that God gives us the opportunity over and over again to tell him our secrets, in our secret places, and to repent for them.

Continue, Beecher, to speak boldly and personally among your people. Never get far away from the certainty of your humanity in their eyes and in their hearts.

Remember that I am continually in prayer for you. My tears are a testimony to my kinship with you and with your struggles. May God's grace abound with you now and always.

Your brother in Christ,
Paul

P.S.: I must confess something to you. Of late, I have been giving much thought to the idea of coming to Washington and preaching in your pulpit. It sounds like a great place to preach! If the Lord permits, I would like to do that? Do you think we could arrange it?

6

BLIND GUIDES AND FOOLISH TEACHERS

PROLOGUE

Washington, D.C.

Dear Paul:

Wow! You really knocked me off my feet with your postscript that time. I do not know how we would make this transfer of time and space, but the pulpit is open to you on any Sunday. (I think some Sundays you really do preach there anyhow!) Any church in the known world would be honored to have you preach. You may not know it, but the prowess of your preaching craft is known in all the churches. And you want me to invite you to Metropolitan? Just say the word!

By the way, Paul, I think I have you at something of a disadvantage when it comes to these epistles and homilies. I notice that you are painstakingly writing yours by stylus, while I am using a computer. It's difficult to describe just what a computer is, but it is a means of gathering all of the words in one instrument that is able not only to record the words but to remember them and then write them for me in a fraction of the time it would take me to do it by hand. I wonder how many letters you would have produced if you had had this kind of help back in the first century. As prolific a writer as you were by hand, heaven help us if you had had a word processor or computer! The detail of information you would have been able to share would have been phenomenal.

On the other hand, our society has become so computer conscious that the church is in danger of developing church memberships which operate only by a computer network, and congregations will soon become a thing of the past. Keep the stylus, Paul. I think we're better off if we keep some things as they were. New is not always better, especially in the church.

The sermon I'm sending this time, Paul, is really a sequel to "I've Got a Secret." In fact, this may be a more biting, stinging sermon than its predecessor. I'm really trying to achieve several things here, Paul.

First, I want to make sure that we who share this calling to the ministry are asking the critical questions of our motives and methods. How easy it is for those of us who are involved in "church work" to fail to examine the quality and the meaning of that work. We in leadership, I think, have the responsibility to ask "Where are we headed?" If we don't know where we're headed, any road we take will get us there. And if we do know where we're headed, it is appropriate to ask, "Who's leading whom?"

The second purpose that I had hoped to achieve was to include laypersons, apart from the ordained ministry, in this effort of evaluation of our spiritual lives, as well as of the churches we are called to serve.

I'm not complaining, Paul, but this is no easy task. When you force the church to ask the difficult questions, it is often misinterpreted. Some fear that you are being overly judgmental, while others feel that any criticism is unwarranted. If the world, however, is asking questions of the church, is it not appropriate that the church ask questions of itself? We who preach this gospel cannot afford the luxury of permitting those who have positions of responsibility to lead us blindly or to teach foolishly. Too much is at stake. Too many lives are being weighed in the balance and found wanting.

I, for one, do not want to look back upon the years of my ministry and discover that I have been a blind guide leading the blind. My record does not nearly match your own, but I have been preaching this gospel for almost three decades, and I would not want to be known as a foolish teacher in heaven.

The tragedy is that most of us engaged in this preaching business never come to an honest assessment of who and what we are, because we continue to measure ourselves by ourselves. We spend the days of our ministry in search of success. When we find what we call success, however, we are often so overwhelmed that we become instead successful failures. What a tragedy! Our memberships are growing; our buildings are expanding; our staff is growing; our income is rising; the church is filled to capacity; we are successful by every standard of excellence known to man, but in the sight of the God who requires more faithfulness than success, we have miserably failed.

You know, Paul, the most devastating thing that can happen to preachers is to discover, when they walk away from the pulpit, that the time was spent preaching to themselves. And it happens time and time again. What a revelation, when that kind of judgment falls. What a revelation that we speak to others of the things we see in ourselves. But what a cleansing to confess that often we are blind guides, often we are foolish teachers. We must learn to be our sternest critics; we must give to ourselves the most severe tests. In so doing we shall keep more faithfully to the course he has set before us.

All the saints here at Washington salute you. Greet Silas and Barnabas and John Mark on our behalf.

Grace and peace,
Beecher

Sermon: BLIND GUIDES AND FOOLISH TEACHERS

Behold, thou art called a Jew, and restest in the law, and makest thy boast of God, And knowest his will, and approvest the things that are more excellent, being instructed out of the law; And art confident that thou thyself art *a guide of the blind,* a light of them which are in darkness, *An instructor of the foolish,* a teacher of babes, which hast the form of knowledge and of the truth in the law (Romans 2:17–20).

Honesty makes me confess that there are some texts of Scripture that preachers would do well to avoid. I would prefer to suggest that while in the process of selecting text and subject, the wise and prudent preacher would do well to remain in the arena of love and grace, redemption and restoration. For, on the other hand, if one insists on trafficking in that arena of sin and judgment, failings and shortcomings, it will not be long before a reversal of sorts takes place and the *preacher* suddenly becomes *the preached to* and *the holder of the light* becomes *the one upon whom the light of questioning and inquisition is cast.*

While in the process of reviewing and examining this Word, I have discovered that the more time one spends in exposing the sins of others, the greater the realization that at the same time and in the same moment one's own sins are equally revealed. Strangely enough, I have discovered that they who handle the two-edged sword of the Word will discover that their own flesh has been scarred and their own blood has been spilled. It is uncomfortable, unbearable, and unavoidable that while in the process of preaching the Word, while in the very act of prophetic proclamation, while in the very motion of "declaring the whole counsel of God," preachers discover that the word they meant for others is a word that is really meant for themselves. Preachers ought to be careful that while they warn others of Satan's fires they may themselves be on their way to hell.

Paul knew of this danger when he wrote the church at Corinth: "I keep under my body, and bring it into subjection:

lest that by any means, when I have preached to others, I myself should be a castaway" (1 Corinthians 9:27).

This word of caution has a ring of contemporary relevance, even though it comes from an ancient setting and circumstance. Paul's writing to the church at Rome is, as you know, the backdrop for this work which is as scathing as it is insightful. While on his way to speak about the justification of sinners, Paul makes it his business to define the nature of sin and the scope of judgment for both the Gentile and the Jew. Paul's theology insists that there is a universality to the matter of sin, so indeed, *"all have sinned, and come short of the glory of God"* (Romans 3:23). More to the point, however, Paul insists that *"there is none righteous, no, not one!"* (3:10).

Let me quickly confess, that when one examines this second chapter of Romans, one cannot be sure precisely to whom it is that Paul is speaking. It is quite obvious that Paul is engaged in conversation; it is a conversation, however, that is more diatribe than dialogue. Here, Paul is engaged in a kind of theological tirade marked by derision and ridicule. What Paul says is that persons who sit in judgment condemn themselves because they are doing the same thing as the one who is being judged. There is no debate that Paul is a Jew addressing Jews, and with this word he seeks to bring to their mind and memory their own sins and shortcomings.

One must not forget that the Jew believed that because he was a Jew . . .

- Simply because of the incidence of his birth as a Jew,
- Simply because he was a descendant of Abraham,
- Simply because it was to the Jews that both law and promise had been given,

the Jew believed that he had preferential status with God.

Paul, on the other hand, took the position that the covenantal relationship which God held with the Jews, did not give them special status or privilege. It did, however, give them special responsibilities. Paul said that there is really not much difference in a Jew who knows the law and does not obey it and a Gentile who never knew the law and therefore should not be expected to obey it.

You must recall that Paul is a Jew writing to Jews. It is, then, as a Jew that he says to them: "You call yourself a Jew? You think you've got it made because you've got the law! And not only that but you brag about your relationship with God and how much you know and how many Bible classes you've attended and how many Sunday School certificates you have plastered on your wall. You just think you've got it made, and the result is that you're arrogant. You think of the Gentiles as blind, and you think it your duty to serve as their guides. You think of the Gentiles as foolish people, and you think it is your responsibility to be their teachers. You tell folk not to steal, and at the same time you're stealing. You tell folk that adultery is wrong and idolatry is wrong, but if I'm not mistaken there's a skeleton or two in your closet."

What Paul is saying, when you get right down to it, is that in order for religion to have any authenticity, in order for religion to have any integrity, at some point or other everybody has to learn to practice what they preach. I assure you that I would not do violence to Paul's writing here, but if you look at it another way, I believe what Paul is saying in essence is that the so-called guides of the blind are actually blind guides and that those who try to teach the foolish are themselves foolish teachers.

Blind Guides and Foolish Teachers

As a matter of analysis you will not find it breaking new exegetical ground when I suggest to you that implicit in Paul's writing is the question: *Who's leading whom?*

There is no doubt in my mind that the twentieth-century church is having questions raised about its identity and its integrity because somebody is asking the question: *Who's leading whom?*

I am convinced that we cannot be entirely certain about the prospects for the church or the future for the church because we cannot adequately answer the question: *Who's leading whom?*

There can be no doubt that those things which have come to mark the contemporary church have ranged from the unbelievable to the outrageous and have rendered the church intellectually and theologically impotent, all because we are uncomfortable with the question: *Who's leading whom?*

In an era when it appears that those of us who claim to know the way have suddenly lost the way and when it appears that those of us who are leading others to the light have suddenly been caught in our own midnight madness, nobody really wants to deal with my question: *Who's leading whom?*

You do recall, of course, that Jesus really raised this same issue that day when the scribes and Pharisees came to him and asked: "Why do thy disciples transgress the tradition of the elders? for they wash not their hands when they eat bread" (Matthew 15:2).

These scribes and Pharisees were hung up on the law. They were busy investigating and holding inquisitions on who was and who was not observing the letter of the law.

Jesus responded to their question saying, "Not that which goeth into the mouth defileth a man; but that which cometh out of the mouth, this defileth a man." In yet another context Jesus said of these same scribes and Pharisees: "Let them alone: they be blind leaders of the blind. And if the blind lead the blind, both shall fall into the ditch" (Matthew 15:14).

I would not make much over little, but it seems to me there is more than a little opportunity for serious tragedy when the blind are leading the blind. For, after all, what is really being suggested here is that because of its condition of blindness, the church is in serious jeopardy and danger.

- After all, this is not just a matter of distorted vision or limited perspective. It's blind men leading blind men.
- After all, this is not just a matter of spiritual cataracts that can be removed by minor surgery. It's blind men leading blind men.
- After all, this is not just a matter of being far-sighted or near-sighted; this is a matter of having *no sight* at all. This is a matter of following those whose only vision is, in the word of James Weldon Johnson, "blacker than a hundred

midnights down in a cypress swamp." It's blind men leading blind men.

If the truth be known, all of us have been blind at sometime. All of us have followed the leading of the blind at sometime. And for those of us who even today are still the blind following the blind, I thought I ought to tell you that Jesus said there's a ditch waiting for you just around the corner.

Now, if you do not mind a brief aside, perhaps I ought to share with you that there is a danger in religious titles. Titles can be treacherous, and I'm not talking about preachers alone. If you are involved in the religious enterprise, if you are involved in a religious lifestyle that puts you in the limelight, you better be careful with your titles. I don't care if you're reverend or doctor or evangelist or Sunday school teacher or elder or deacon or trustee or usher or president or chairman; if you've got the responsibility for leading somebody in the name of Christ, you better be careful with the titles by which you are called, because before you know it somebody could discover that as far as the integrity of your ministry or your service is concerned, it's really just the blind leading the blind, and the foolish teaching the foolish.

When the blind are leading the blind and the foolish are teaching the foolish something happens—I'm not certain what it is, but something happens—as a result of this unfortunate leadership arrangement. The first thing that occurs whenever the world discovers who's leading whom is that it *calls into question the authenticity of our conversion experience.*

We live in an era when it has become vogue, it has become popular to tell people "I am a born-again Christian." I am a child of the church, and the first thing I remember folk saying about their religious experience was, "I'm saved and sanctified, free from sin and born again." I remember going to church for what they used to call Covenant Meetin', and the first hour was spent by those telling how they "met the Lord" and how the Lord had turned their life around.

We're not far from that era, for there is still somebody here today who could testify right now that one day the Lord "picked your feet out of the miry clay, set your feet on a solid rock, and established your goings." There's somebody here today like the apostle Paul who could testify that one day the Lord knocked you down, but he "picked you up and turned you around." No doubt there are those in the church today who may not be familiar with the language of the church in days gone by but who, in their own manner, would live out the testimony of the sure hand of God who has given a new and abundant life.

When, however, the blind are leading the blind and the foolish are leading the foolish, the world has questions about the authenticity and the integrity of that experience which is so central to our spiritual lives.

When the world sees that the blind are leading the blind and the foolish are teaching the foolish, it draws into critical question the reliability of the faith we claim and proclaim in the name of Jesus who is the Christ.

What I'm trying to say is: When the lives we lead are contradictory to the faith we proclaim, not only is the meaning of our salvation called into question, but the world becomes concerned about the sincerity with which we claim to have been saved.

Something happens when the blind are leading the blind and the foolish are teaching the foolish.

Perhaps the second thing that happens is that *we participate in a process of self-deception.* Van B. Weigel in his book entitled *Ostrich Christianity* has suggested that we may be dealing with an absurd deception in what he calls "popular Christianity."

Self-deception. We deceive ourselves by adopting and perpetuating certain patterns of perception which obscure both the relevant and the real. If we consider ourselves above and beyond sin, we deceive ourselves. If we try to convince the world that we are holier-than-thou, we deceive ourselves. If we want others to believe that there are no stains on our garments and no dirty linen in our closets, we deceive ourselves.

We don't have to rise very high in the church before we contract ecclesiastical egoitis. Just get elected president or get appointed chairman, and before you know it we're carrying

Bibles and wearing crosses and every other word is "Praise the Lord!" It doesn't take us long not only to get righteous but to get self-righteous. And that's why I read 1 John 1:8: "If we say that we have no sin, we deceive ourselves, and the truth is not in us."

Something happens when the blind lead the blind and when the foolish teach the foolish.

Perhaps the third thing that happens is that *we forget that somebody is following us.* It ought to be a sobering, solemn thought to realize that every day of your life somebody is following you. It's not the newspaper, it's not the five o'clock news, it's not the FBI or the CIA, but somebody is following you. Somebody is following your example. Somebody is following your footsteps. Somebody is trying to talk like you talk and walk like you walk. And the problem is that there is really no way for your to realize how many lives you are influencing.

Fathers ought to realize that there is a child that is following. Mothers ought to realize that there is a daughter that wants to walk in your high heel shoes. Teachers must provide the role models. Parents, you must provide a pattern for your children that will let them know there is something else in life other than following Michael Jackson doing the "moon walk" and saying, "I'm bad, you know it, I'm bad!"

Our children need new heroes in a culture where the permanent has been replaced by the plastic and where society is now secondary to computers and gallium arseride. But when the blind are leading the blind and the foolish are teaching the foolish, it's mighty easy to forget that somebody is following you.

Something happens when the blind are leading the blind. Perhaps what happens is that *we tend to forget that the student is always the mirror image of the teacher.*

Let me see if I can make this plain:

- If there is something wrong with the church,
- If there is something wrong with these persons we call Christians,

112

- If those who claim to be part of the Christian cause are at the same time inconsistent in their Christian conduct,
- If those who make up the church can be rightfully accused of simply putting on an "outside show for an unfriendly world,"
- If those who walk in the church are more concerned about who sees them when they walk down the aisle than they are about the quality of their walk with God,
- If there is some dread sickness which has taken up residence in the body of Christ and has taken on epidemic proportions,
- If "the acorn never falls far from the oak tree,"
- If the student is the mirror image of the teacher,

it may be that the church is in the condition that it is in because those of us who have set the pace and made the mold and charted the course have been no more than the blind leading the blind.

It's convicting to me to confess that I may have culpability for the condition of the church. If a preacher's people are the product of his or her preaching and yet when they look out on Sunday morning and realize that the sick have not been healed, the wounded have not been made whole, sinners have not been converted, lives have not been changed—there is judgment on those of us who wear these robes and stand in lofty places. Could it be the blind leading the blind?

I assure you I do not mean to offend my colleagues; I don't intend to aggravate or annoy my brothers and my sisters of the cloth, but when I realize that maybe I have not done what I should have done, and maybe I have not said what I should have said, and maybe I have not been what I should have been, that's the time when you'll hear me saying:

> Have Thine own way, Lord,
> Have Thine own way.
> Thou art the potter, I am the clay.
> Melt me and mold me after Thy will,
> While I am waiting, yielded and still.

When the blind lead the blind and when the foolish teach the foolish, that's the time when somebody needs to say a word about forgiveness.

- You may think that you can live without sin, and yet you cannot. We need forgiveness.
- You may think that you can afford to live in a glass house, and yet you cannot. We need forgiveness.
- You may think that you can sit in judgment on everybody else, and yet you cannot. We need forgiveness.

Consider the dialogue of Judgment and Forgiveness:
- Judgment says, "Your sins will find you out."
- But Forgiveness says, "Though your sins be as scarlet they shall be as wool; though they be red like crimson they shall be white as snow."

- Judgment says, "The wages of sin is death."
- But Forgiveness says: "The gift of God is eternal life."

The ultimate lesson of blind guides and foolish teachers is that because we want forgiveness, we have learned how to be forgiving.

Because we want forgiveness, we don't judge others because one day others will judge us.

Because we want to be forgiven, we have learned how to love our enemies and pray for those who persecute us and despitefully use us.

Because we want to be forgiven when our brother is overtaken in a fault we will hurry up and get those who are spiritual minded to restore him because we know we can also be tempted.

The gospel in all of this is that if you find yourself being taught by a foolish teacher, or if you find yourself being led by a blind leader, don't despair. God has already fixed it so that you can have another leader. When I am blind I have another leader.

What kind of leader do you have, preacher? The Great Shepherd who is the Shepherd's Shepherd, he is my leader. He of whom David sang, who leads me in paths of righteousness for his namesake, he is my leader. He who knows the way because he is the Way, he is my leader. Yes, he's my leader!

> He leadeth me, O blessed thought!
> O words with heavenly comfort fraught!
> Whate'er I do, where'er I be,
> Still 'tis God's hand that leadeth me.

> He leadeth me, He leadeth me,
> By his own hand He leadeth me;
> His faithful follower I would be,
> For by hand He leadeth me.

EPILOGUE

Thessolonica

Beecher, my brother:

It is about one-thirty in the morning, and I cannot seem to get myself to sleep. Young man, you have disturbed my soul. I have a copy of "Blind Guides and Foolish Teachers" in one hand and my letter to those at Rome in the other. Here I am, shaking my head, wondering if I am a foolish teaching apostle, or if I am blindly being guided (or assaulted?) by the words which fell from my own mouth and which were passed down by my pen.

How I long to have one of those computers of which you speak! I could use it to respond both to your letter and to your sermon more quickly. Writing is so much harder for me now that my sight continues to fail me. (By the way, are you really sure that computers are not the instrument of Satan? With anything that good, there must be something wrong!) Nevertheless, I remain strong in the Lord and in the power of his might, knowing that he will provide for my need according to his riches. Strangely enough, Beecher, as my body grows weaker, my faith grows stronger.

Your letter, Beecher, has caused me to meditate on my own conversion. My conversion is one of the few certainties in my life, Beecher, and yet your interpretation of these passages has caused me to pray for new assurance that I am leading those called to be saints as our Lord would want me to.

Sermons like this one are what I call "God's quality control department." Preachers who are not called to account for their ministries are like arrows shot indiscriminately into the air, with no concern for their direction or the harm their misdirection might create. There must be some system of personal and professional accountability lest we come to deserve these harsh titles and more.

On the other hand, Beecher, have you lost your mind? No one wants to hear these kinds of sermons. Laypersons are confused by them and preachers think they are above them. By what authority do you speak to your peers in this manner? And what makes you think that this "boomerang" sermon which came from me and then turned and came back to me is going to ingratiate you with me? You have some nerve! In my idiom you have some <u>chutzpah</u>! I thought Peter and John preached "boldly" in the Lord. I think you are trying to bring a new definition to this kind of "holy boldness."

To speak openly and honestly with you, I am aware that those of us who preach and teach have been called to the ministry of leadership. How painfully aware we are that the responsiblity of walking upright, as God would have us do, is sometimes (<u>all</u> the time?) a heavy burden. When we falter the people forget that we too are God's children, just as they are. The difference is that God has set us apart. He has called us to his service. He has anointed us with his Holy Spirit, and our only power to preach is the power we gain through him.

Beecher, it is amazing the power words have to paint a picture on the canvas of one's mind. Can you see the utter confusion, depression, and dismay that would come from the circumstance of the blind leading the blind? It is the same confusion and depression and dismay which occurs when those who teach the Scriptures are unfamiliar with it and uncaptivated by it.

So perhaps I am a foolish teacher. (I'll take this from you, but I don't like it!) However, Beecher, if I am a foolish teacher I still know what I know. I am not so arrogant as to believe that all Christian teaching begins and ends with me. I can only boast of one thing: Jesus Christ, the cross at Calvary, and the resurrection on Easter Sunday morning. If that makes me a foolish teacher and the saints blind-guided, then so be it!

I know this as well, young man. Judgment will find us all out. Right? Right!

Pax!
Paul

7

THE STIGMA
OF BEING HOLY

PROLOGUE

Washington

Dear Paul:

I received your letter and was overjoyed to know
that you are yet strong in the Lord. God be praised
that even though your eyesight fails your insight is as
keen and sharp as ever. You must know how earnestly
we pray for you day and night and how our faith is
increased day by day because of the Word of faith
which you preach and because of the faith which is so
pronounced in these letters of ours.

There is one thing, Paul, I must share with you
now. Understand that I have not kept it from you or in
any manner tried to deceive you, but the necessity to
bring it up has not surfaced until now. I am a
preacher of African descent, and the people whom I
serve have a similar cultural heritage. Most of us can
trace our lineage to the shores of western Africa. Four
hundred years ago our ancestors were trapped and
placed in huge ships and brought to this country. We
left our homeland as princes, kings, and queens. When
we arrived here we were divided from our families, our
language was confused, our religion was repressed, and
we were made to serve as slaves to our oppressors.

We are convinced that no other people have been made to serve in such a demeaning fashion on this order in the whole of human history. In fact, though we are now legally free, the system of slavery is still intact, though the oppressor has given it new names such as "welfare" and the like.

I wanted to share this with you, Paul (I realize that you are personally acquainted with servitude, and I bring to mind even now your compassion with the circumstance of Philemon and Onesimus), because our history involves the repression of our religious life as well. When we came from our native home our drums were taken away, and we were no longer permitted to dance. For us, in the native homelands from which we came to this region, religion consumed the whole of life, and a religion without rejoicing and celebration was for us a contradiction in terms. The Christians at Rome worshiped in houses and in catacombs, but our people, during days of the harshest slavery known to man, worshiped in brush arbors and shanties down by the riverside.

Because our language was confused (members of the same tribe usually did not live on the same plantation), our method of worship of the High God was destroyed. We learned how to sing by listening to our Anglo-Saxon masters and memorizing the words without their knowing. We even memorized the Scripture, and God spoke to some of our foreparents and gave them the gifts of interpretation and preaching, and they discovered that what the masters were teaching and preaching was distorted and untrue. When they discovered what God really said through his Word, and when they did have an opportunity to worship him freely and fully, to say it succinctly, they brought a new definition to the word celebration.

I have given you all this background history so I can ask a question, Paul. Do you know what it is to "shout"? Have you ever been so caught up in the Spirit that you could not keep still and you could not keep quiet? Have you ever been so overcome by the powerful presence of Christ in your life that you clapped your hands or did some strange walking and running or lifted holy hands or found some other means of praise over which you really had no control? Well, this shouting business is something to which many of our people are given. (Regrettably, fewer and fewer are given to it these days. We've become so educated and sophistocated and urbanized that we don't have time for this kind of activity anymore!)

Perhaps I am going on far too much about all of this, but I thought you needed to know about this phenomenon of praise, because it has a direct link to the concept of holiness with which you were so greatly concerned when you wrote to the Christian community at Rome. We are still wrestling and trying to come to terms with the meaning of the word holiness. For many it is a kind of spiritual lifestyle which tends toward perfection, or at least the claim of perfection. Very often those who are either holy or trying their best to become holy are those who are given to moments of extended spiritual ecstacy and praise.

So here comes another one, Paul. I heard what you said about this issue of holiness, and I think I have understood you properly, but if not I sure would appreciate a more definitive word from you. You know, it's hard to be holy—pure, clean, perfect; at the same time I wonder if we spend too much time at this praise business. When you went to church was it quiet all the time, or was there ever any audible voluminous praise connected with your worship? Some of us are really trying to be holy as you suggest, but the concept is so vague as to be impossible to achieve.

Through all of this, Paul, we continue steadfast, always abounding in the work of the Lord. We continue to pray for you and implore you to pray for us that we might be the vessels of praise which he requires in these last and evil days.

Grace and peace, my brother,
Beecher

Sermon: THE STIGMA OF BEING HOLY

As ye have yielded your members servants to uncleanness and to iniquity unto iniquity; even so now yield your members servants to righteousness unto holiness (Romans 6:19).

Depending upon the perception of one's religious experience, it may come as something of a shock to discover that even in the church of Jesus Christ it is difficult, if not impossible, to find anyone that is legitimately and authentically *holy*. Biblically, of course, there is little doubt or debate that holiness or purity or sanctification or blamelessness or saintliness—what the Greeks call *hagiasmos*—there is no doubt that holiness is both the aim and the goal of religion, but I, for one, have not encountered too many who have so met the mark or so reached the goal that they can properly be identified or who deserve to be identified as holy.

To be sure . . .

- There are some who have made some as yet unsubstantiated claims regarding their holiness.
- There are some who have spent long hours cultivating the *appearance* of holiness.
- There are some whose length of years in membership with religious institutions would lead one to suspect that by now at least they *ought* to be holy.

And yet, I am of the opinion that despite all of this, even in the church of Jesus Christ it is difficult, if not impossible, to find anyone that is legitimately and authentically *holy!*

I raise this issue primarily because I am concerned about what appears to be an absence of holiness and an absence of those who are themselves holy within the institutional church as we know it.

It disturbs me that for some reason the contemporary church seems unable to produce or to reproduce in its adherents that which it was designed to create.

It disturbs me that as we come to the close of the twentieth century, what one is more likely to find in the church is not *holy Christians* but a rather peculiar contradiction in terms: people who prefer to be Christians of the amorphous, generic kind without any requirement for being authentically holy.

It disturbs me that very often we who represent the Holy, we who are claimed and called by the Holy, we who say we have been convicted and converted to a lifestyle that is in its essence holy, we who sing of the Trinity (the triune manifestation of the Eternal) and in so doing cry out "Holy, Holy, Holy!"—it disturbs me that we are not ourselves holy.

It disturbs me that even though God's Word speaks of holiness and defines holiness and requires holiness, it disturbs me that there are not too many preachers who are preaching about holiness and, as a result, not too many church folk who are living in the path and pattern of holiness.

In fact, . . .

- Just to talk about holiness causes some to be uncomfortable.
- Just to bring up the holiness issue causes an increased anxiety level in some.
- Just to hold a conversation regarding the holiness concept can turn some off.

I have discovered that even those who might have a legitimate claim to being holy tend to keep it quiet and don't really tell anybody if they suspect that they are holy.

Evidently, there is something wrong with being holy. Evidently there is some difficulty in dealing with this matter of holiness in the pulpit as well as in the pew. Evidently, the idea of holiness conjures up some notions and gives rise to certain attitudes and causes some intellectual and philosophical problems among those who ought to be committed to the habit of holiness.

You are aware, of course, that this matter of holiness is not my idea. Contrary to popular belief, holiness is not an option.

- The Scripture teaches that God's people are, by definition, a holy people and a holy nation. Leviticus 20:7 says, *"Sanctify yourselves therefore, and be ye holy!"*
- The Scripture teaches that the tithe is holy.
- The Psalms say that the place for worship is at his holy hill.
- When Isaiah was ordained, the angel touched his lips with coals of fire from the altar and cried, "HOLY!"
- The Scripture teaches that the temple of God is holy, and David says that holiness becomes his house.
- God gave Moses the Law and told him to remember the Sabbath day and keep it holy.
- Paul told Timothy that God calls us with a holy calling, and not only that, but if you're going to praise the Lord, you have to lift up holy hands.

God's name is holy: "Bless the Lord, O my soul: and all that is within me, bless his holy name."

Even this word which we preach was written by holy men who were inspired by the Holy Ghost.

At a biblical level it is clear that the concepts of the holy and holiness are part and parcel of what relevant religion and authentic Christianity are all about.

It may be appropriate then, with at least a brief understanding of holiness as a biblical basis for our discussion and dialogue, to take a momentary glance at this rather obscure and obtuse text written, as you know, by the hand of the apostle Paul. This note on iniquity and holiness, which comes from the hand of an aging apostle whose days are indeed numbered, does not, I will admit, usually provide proper kindling for preaching fire. And yet here is Paul writing from Corinth with love to those whom he says are "called to be saints."

You must understand that these are the ones to whom Paul writes: captives in the catacombs of a culture capitulated to sin.

- These are the ones to whom Paul writes: citizens of a commonwealth of hitherto unknown corruption and dereliction.
- These are the ones to whom Paul writes: Jews and Gentiles, Greeks and Barbarians, the wise and the unwise.
- These are the ones to whom Paul writes: those who live daily amid the debauchery of Roman hedonism, narcissism, perverted sexuality, and homosexuality.
- These are the ones who live in that city of the caesars set on seven hills where the sun of God's morality has been eclipsed by the midnight of man's immorality, where virtue has lost out to vice, where goodness has given way to greed, and where weakness has degenerated to wickedness.

To these, the unclean, the impure, the iniquitous, the defiled, the dirty, the weak and the wicked—to these, Paul says:

YIELD YOUR MEMBERS SERVANTS TO RIGHTEOUSNESS UNTO HOLINESS.

Distilled to its essence, what Paul is addressing here is the manner by which sinners can escape the power of sin. It is here in this very same passage (v. 23) that Paul reminds his readers that *"the wages of sin is death."* Paul is saying, then, that once a man is converted that which he *was* is no longer what he *is*. The converted man once was a servant of sin. But now that a change has taken place, and now that one has (so to speak) acquired a brand new walk, we are no longer servants of sin but servants of righteousness.

The process of moving from sin to salvation, the process of moving from what I used to be to what God wants me to be, the process of moving from the old me to the new me, is achieved by means of a deliberate, cognitive, reasoned decision. Once I yielded my body to uncleanness and iniquity, but now I have *decided* to yield my body to righteousness unto holiness.

In other words, one does not just stumble upon holiness. One does not locate sanctification by chance or holiness by accident. Paul insists that if you seek or desire the fruits of holiness, the gift of God through holiness, then you must decide to give up, to surrender, to yield your bodies "servants to righteousness unto holiness." It was within this same connection that Paul gave his classic word of advise on the holiness concept:

> I beseech you therefore, brethren,
> by the mercies of God,
> that ye present your bodies a living sacrifice,
> holy, acceptable unto God!
>
> (Romans 12:1)

The result of this argumentation is to encourage a closer examination of what I call *the stigma of being holy* because evidently there are some *dangers inherent in the claim of holiness.*

By way of analysis then it appears that *the first danger of holiness is that it is difficult to be holy.* Honesty makes us confess that it's hard to be clean when you reside in an unclean world. It's hard to walk the "straight and narrow" when you have to function in a world of six- and eight-lane highways and when every road leads to "brighter lights" and "bigger cities." Even if one wanted to be "straight-laced" and "prim and proper," it's hard to pull it off in a "let-your-hair-down" society.

- It's hard to live holy when you have to live in an unholy environment.
- It's hard to live holy when every day you have to live in hell.
- It's hard to be holy when you have to work for the devil himself.
- It's hard to hold your tongue when the very hounds of hell are on your trail.
- Maybe then the danger of holiness is simply that it is difficult to be holy.

But to look closer still, one discovers that the primary danger of holiness is that *some may question the authenticity or the integrity of your claim.* Before you claim to be holy, you better be sure you can back it up. I wouldn't tell anybody how sanctified you are if you've still got dirty linen in your closet. If I were you, I wouldn't put on to be so "holier-than-thou" if I still had residence in a glass house. I'd be careful because, just as soon as you get through testifying—you know how we testify:

Child, I know I'm free from sin,
washed in the blood, sanctified,
regenerated, fire baptized,
filled with the Holy Ghost
and born again!

Just as soon as you get through testifying, somebody is going to check you out!

You see, there's a fine line between *testifying* and *"testalying."* Be careful with how holy you claim to be because somebody wants to know if you're walking that walk or just talking that talk. When it comes to testifying, I'd rather just tell somebody:

I'M A SINNER SAVED BY GRACE!

I believe that's a pretty good testimony because it's dangerous to claim to be holy if you cannot back up the integrity of your claim.

But there's more than a danger with regard to this matter of holiness. There is a stigma. There is an uncompromising and uncomplimentary mark that is attached to those who are a part of the holiness crowd. When anyone makes a claim to holiness they are *immediately perceived as having some form of mental imbalance.* Whenever people give themselves over to the religious process, when the priorities of Christ become life-consuming or when they begin to view things with a spiritual mind rather than a carnal mind, there comes a suspicion that something is wrong with their mental apparatus.

There is a notion afoot that in order for one to be holy one must be intellectually irresponsible. You remember, that was the problem Nicodemus had with this matter of being saved and born again. Nicodemus said "this 'born-again' business is academically, genetically, and biologically indefensible. How can a man be born when he is old? Shall he enter a second time into his mother's womb?"

Jesus responded by saying, "Nicodemus, that's not the only thing you don't understand. You hear the wind but you don't know who gave the wind its breath. Oh, yes, you feel the wind but you don't know where the wind came from or where the wind is going. But just because you don't understand it doesn't mean it isn't so."

Isaiah said, "There is no searching of his understanding."

Job said he does "great things past finding out. . .and wonders without number."

In fact, his ways are not our ways and his thoughts are not our thoughts.

One's religion does not have to be intellectually irresponsible in order for one to pursue a life of holiness.

You see:
- It's my sense that gives me soul.
- It's my faith that gives me feeling.

In fact, I don't want a religion that turns on my feeling but shuts off my brain.
- It's my regenerated intellect that tells me what's real.
- It's my baptized brain that tells me what to believe.
- It's my consecrated cerebellum that gives me something to hold on to.
- It's my sanctified psyche that gives me something to shout about!

Not only are those who claim to be holy perceived as though they are mentally imbalanced, but in point of fact, *they are perceived as religious fanatics.* I can recall a time not too long ago when folk in the Baptist church did not want to be connected with Holiness or Apostolic or Pentecostal or storefront people because the kind of ecstatic, chrarismatic, shouting religion that they practiced was beneath their social rank. Because the so-called Holiness church was the storefront church or the "little church" and the Baptist church or the Methodist church was the "big church," the folk in the big church looked down their noses at the folk in the little church. I was reared in an era when folk didn't make too much noise in church because somehow you might be associated with those

127

"holy roller" people. We did not applaud in church. And in some other churches (whose names I shall not mention in present company) you didn't say "Amen" too loudly.

And don't talk about musical instruments! We had no drums. For God's sake, no tambourine. No bass. No violin. Because if you participated in all of that, you'd be branded as a religious fanatic.

But I'm glad today that somebody discovered that if the Lord has rescued you, somebody ought to say something.

- If the Lord has brought you from a mighty long way, somebody ought to say something.
- If the Lord has helped you raise those children, somebody ought to say something.
- If the Lord has opened doors for you that no man can shut, somebody ought to say something.
- If the Lord has been a bridge over troubled waters, somebody ought to say something.

The redeemed of the Lord ought to say so!

- Who cares how prim and proper you are? Say something.
- Who cares how sophisticated you are? Say something.
- Who cares how many degrees you have? Say something.
- Who cares what side of town you live on? When you've got tears that meet up under your chin and the Lord wipes every tear from your eyes, say something.
- Who cares if you don't like noise in church? I feel sorry for you. If you don't like noise in church, don't go to heaven!

> When all God's children get to heaven,
> what a time, what a time, what a time!

It won't be very long and you'll have an eternity to be quiet. But for right now, say something!

And, just in case you don't like the new trend toward contemporary music and the use of instruments in worship, I talked to David about it. David said:

> Praise him with the trumpet,
> Praise him with the psaltery and harp,

Praise him with the timbrel and dance,
Praise him with stringed instruments and organ,
Praise him with the loud cymbals,
Praise him with the high-sounding cymbals,
Let everything that hath breath
Praise the Lord!

Is that what it means to be a religious fanatic? I don't know whether praising the Lord will make you a religious fanatic or not, but I do know that *it's easier to cool off a religious fanatic than it is to heat up a religious corpse.*

The Scripture reveals that they had some fanatics in Jerusalem one day. It was on that day when men came from every nation and they met up in an old upper room. They had so many in church *that* morning they had to put chairs in the aisle. Just as soon as they got there, they tell me, there "came a sound from heaven as of a rushing mighty wind and it filled all the house where they were sitting. And there appeared unto them cloven tongues like as of fire, and it sat upon each of them."

These religious fanatics were so holy that Luke says they were filled with the Holy Ghost and began to speak with other tongues as the spirit gave them utterance. I believe the church needs a little more wind and a little more fire. The church needs the wind of the Spirit that will blow through every once in a while and turn things upside down and right-side up. The church needs the fire of the Holy Ghost that will set things on hallowed fire, a fire that will run from heart to heart and from breast to breast.

In the last analysis, the stigma of being holy is not really to be found in the matter of mental imbalance, it is not really to be found in the matter of religious fanaticism. The stigma of being holy has to do with the fact that *we have ill defined what holiness is and what holiness is not.* We must be careful here for everything that looks and sounds and shouts like holiness is not necessarily holiness.

▪ Holiness is not about what you wear; holiness is about how you walk.

- Holiness is not about the cross you wear; holiness is about the cross you bear.
- Holiness is not about the Bible you carry; holiness is about the Bible that carries you.
- Holiness is not about how well you preach; holiness is about how well you pray.
- Holiness is not about whether you're an officer; holiness is about whether you're a witness.
- Holiness is not about the quantity of your tithe; holiness is about the quality of your life.
- Holiness is not about how high you lift your hands; holiness is about how high you lift your fellowman.
- Holiness is not about how high you jump when you shout; holiness is about how well you serve when you come back down.

I must finally confess that I really want to have a holiness church. In fact, I don't want to be associated with a church that is not a holiness church. If God is holy, his church ought to be holy. He's coming back for his church one day, and he said it ought to be without spot or wrinkle. I want a holy church.

Moses made his way up Mount Sinai one day and there God let him see the fire burn. They tell me the bush burned, but it was not consumed. And I heard God tell Moses, "Take the shoes from off thy feet for the place wherein thou standest is holy ground."

When I come to God's house I want to stand on holy ground. I want Metropolitan to be holy ground.

- When you come to pray, I want you to pray on holy ground.
- When the choir stands to sing, I want the choir to sing on holy ground.
- When sinners are saved, I want them to be saved on holy ground.
- When saints take their flight to worlds unknown, I want them to go home from holy ground.

> I'm pressing on the upward way,
> New heights I'm gaining every day—

Still praying as I'm onward bound,
"Lord, plant my feet on higher ground."

My heart has no desire to stay
Where doubts arise and fears dismay;
Though some may dwell where these abound,
My prayer, my aim, is higher ground.

I want to scale the utmost height
And catch a gleam of glory bright;
But still I'll pray till heav'n I've found,
"Lord, lead me on to higher ground."

Lord, lift me up and let me stand
By faith, on heaven's tableland;
A higher plane than I have found—
Lord, plant my feet on higher ground.

EPILOGUE

Galatia

Dear Beecher, my brother beloved in the gospel of Christ:

You really do know how to provide surprises. To be quite honest with you, I had never given thought to your cultural background. You see, my brother, those who have been absorbed in the Christ-life are the first to abandon cultural distinctions. After all, we will not gain or be denied entrance into the kingdom of God based on our ethnic background. I celebrate the noble heritage out of which you have come. The loins of your ancestors through civilizations that pre-date Christ have paved the way for mankind to acknowledge him who is the creator of us all.

You recall, by the way, that during the persecution of Herod the Great, Jesus was spirited away to Africa for a period of hiding. Jesus has always been linked with people whose color has often occasioned their oppression and their pain. Your insights about the spiritual development of your people have been helpful to me; it has also given me some helpful clues regarding the authority and the freedom of your preaching. Let God be praised for the freedom he has given to us in spite of the objections of the evil one.

I do long to be with you, however, if for no other reason than to be able to see the expression on your face when you make certain statements. I am not always sure whether you are serious or poking fun. Just what is it that makes you think that people of African descent have the corner on shouting and praising God?

Do you really want to know if we ever shout? Have you ever figured out what those people were doing on that Sunday Jesus rode into town on that donkey, with people climbing trees, waving palms, and singing wildly in the streets? That was a shout! Have you ever figured out (you see, I am beginning to write repetitively as you often do! I must break bad habits!) what the ruckus was on Pentecost Sunday? And do you remember when Silas and I were in jail, and he started singing and I started praying? What do you think caused the earthquake? No, my son, the Lord's people have been shouting for a long time, and I trust they will for a long time to come.

I dare say the stigma attached to being holy has been around for quite some time as well. Obviously, it was felt when I wrote from Corinth to Rome. To tell you the truth, Beecher, I wondered after my Damascus Road experience if I was in my right mind. Consider my dilemma. For years I had been a student of the law. I had been taught by no less a one than Gamaliel, a doctor of the law. I was a Pharisee among Pharisees. But then to be completely cut off from all of it by Someone whom I had never before encountered who called my name and changed my name and made me act and think in ways that were foreign to my heritage, my training, and my rearing — I must honestly confess that I questioned my sanity.

Now, Beecher, the real stigma of being holy is that if it is real (or as you would say, if it is authentic), it is always on public display. One cannot hide or camouflage holiness. Can you *imagine what the people thought when they saw Saul — that old rigid, conservative, hide-bound, dyed-in-the-wool, archenemy of anything or anyone or any movement that was anti-Jewish — can you imagine what they thought or what they said when I went into the synogogue to preach and to teach about Jesus? Can you see the expressions of disbelief and rage in their eyes as I began to proclaim his messiahship and declare him to be the very Son of God? Beecher, the Jews in Damascus were ready to kill me. But thanks to the <u>stigma</u> — that Holy Ghost stigma — there were those who rose to my defense just in the nick of time.*

God is my witness that I am not ashamed of my <u>stigma,</u> and I perceive that you are not ashamed of your own. It occurs to me also, my son in the gospel, that there is an even more important and pervasive stigma to which you allude – the stigma of "trying to be holy"! Yet, we must continue steadfast, and we must continue to encourage those who are given to us to remain steadfast. Life can change. Life can be better. We need not remain subservient to sin for the balance of our days. Just as we once were slaves to the wickedness of this life, so can we now become slaves and servants to his righteousness for holy purposes. As we are slaves to his holiness we are free to be holy in this life, yea even in the life everlasting which is to come.

Grace and peace be with you always, my brother beloved in the Lord. Greet your sons and your daughter and your fair and beloved wife, Elizabeth. I continue daily to pray their blessing and their strength in the Lord Christ.

A stigmatized servant,
Paul

8

THE TRAGEDY OF A PSYCHOTIC PREACHER

PROLOGUE

Washington, D.C.

Paul, my brother in Christ Jesus!

This letter comes to you on the wings of fear and trembling. It is my latest attempt at understanding who preachers are, who you are, and what makes Paul Paul.

I have written of you and preached about you in love. I anxiously await your response.

Grace and peace,
Beecher

P.S.: I realize, Paul, that one of the great risks I am taking here is in the very strong language of the title of the sermon itself. I am aware, as you are, that there is an immense difference between neurosis and psychosis, and I really don't mean to imply that you or other preachers are violently crazy. Or are they?

Sermon: THE TRAGEDY OF A PSYCHOTIC PREACHER

For I know that in me (that is, in my flesh,) dwelleth no good thing: for to will is present with me; but how to perform that which is good I find not. For the good that I would I do not: but the evil which I would not, that I do (Romans 7:18–19).

By and large, as a matter of personal discretion and professional ethics, preachers should rarely write or speak of other preachers, and seldom, if ever, should they write or speak of themselves. This is primarily so, I suspect, because there is a kind of double jeopardy which may occur when the reverse is true. The preacher who writes or speaks of other preachers may be cast in a critical or judgmental light and, on the other hand, the preachers who write about themselves may be found guilty of those flights of fantasy or, if you will, those escapades of ego with which not a few preachers have already been identified.

Until days of recent vintage, preachers did not speak of other preachers in public places lest someone hearing might not hear with a sympathetic ear or understand with an empathetic heart. It has not been until days of recent vintage, I tell you, that preachers have dared speak of themselves. For to speak publically and personally of self is to run the risk that sins will be seen, faults will be found, digressions will be discovered, and moral lapses will be revealed.

On the other hand, the image of the preacher—*who the preacher is or what the preacher is not*—is a subject of common controversy and debate. Gather any crowd together and there is always some interesting talk about the preacher that ranges from high praise on the one hand to low estimation on the other. No matter how long the preacher has been around most people are not sure who the preacher is. They *see* the preacher, but they are not sure *of* the preacher. They *hear* the preacher, but they're not sure if they *understand* what he or she is saying.

After all, who is the preacher anyhow?

Who is this one who dares to speak in the name of the Almighty? Who is this one who dares to stand in the presence of God and declare that among all others, God has chosen to speak directly to them. Who is this one we call "Preacher"?

- Is this person man or myth?
- Prophet or puppet?
- Paradigm or paradox?
- Saint or sinner?
- Conversion artist or just a con artist?

- Holy man or hustler?
- Spiritual shepherd or ecclesiastical pimp?
- Missionary or mercenary?
- Is this person the one to whom God's people ought to bring their tithes and offerings, or is the preacher, in fact, just stealing in the name of the Lord?

Make no mistake about it, I am among them—these persons called preachers. While I share these thoughts with you, I cannot claim ecclesiastical exemption or exception from this work of searching judgment, scathing analysis, and personal introspection. It is not my intention to antagonize my peers and fellow sufferers. By the same token, we preachers have looked at others and their sins. Maybe now we ought to look at preachers and their sins.

After all, . . .
- Robes can't hide us.
- Backward collars can't shield us.

And, anyhow, preachers tend to be so moody and temperamental, so pietistic and presumptuous and pompous that maybe we ought to just look at who preachers really are.

Maybe there is a psychosis in the pew that has its genesis in the pulpit.

Maybe there's a sickness in the sanctuary for which preachers are personally responsible and professionally culpable.

Perhaps there is justifiable cause to examine what I have come to call the "Tragedy of a Psychotic Preacher."

I dare to raise this issue of the personality traits of the preacher, even though there is a clear and present danger in doing so. On its face this idea, this concept, this notion of a psychotic preacher appears to be paradoxical if not a clear contradiction in terms. Fundamentally, one does not associate the word *preacher* with the word *psychotic*.

- Preachers are called.
- Preachers are chosen.
- Preachers are anointed.
- Preachers are pillars of the community.

• Preachers are perched on the pillars and pedestals of popularity.

How then can these words—*preacher* and *psychotic*—be related?

By way of textual analysis, it is appropriate to suggest that there is biblical precedent for the argument we put forth. The biblical student is aware, of course, that for the first six chapters of Paul's epistle to the church at Rome, Paul has gone to extensive lengths to describe the nature and the penalty of sin. Paul has insisted that secret sins will be revealed and—for those who persist—he has suggested as well that "the wages of sin is death."

For the first six chapters Paul has suggested that even though the gospel is the "power of God unto salvation to everyone that believeth," he still insists that only "the just shall live by faith." Moreover, this converted rabbi from Tarsus has suggested that those who claim a Christian allegiance must "yield [their] bodies servants to righteousness unto holiness."

But here in the seventh chapter, the preacher becomes the patient. After all Paul's tirades against sin and degradation, he who speaks of sin becomes the focus of sin. Suddenly and without warning, the bold lines he once had drawn are bold no more. The yardstick the preacher used to measure others is now used against himself. The word of judgment that once sounded from a certain trumpet now issues a sound that is nearly muffled and nearly mute. Here is a preacher who had discovered the hard way the danger of singing "Shine on Me!" as the light from the "lighthouse" has illuminated those areas of his life that were previously hidden and protected from the inspection of public scrutiny and review.

Says Paul:
• I have discovered something in myself.
• I have discovered that I am not what I thought I was.
• I thought I had it together.
• I thought I was emotionally secure.
• I thought I was on firm psychological soil.

137

- But now I have discovered that there is a *new me* and an *old me*. Everytime I think I have the *new me* lined up, the *old me* shows up.

Not only that—there is a war going on.
- My mind is at odds with my members.
- My carnality is at conflict with my spirituality.
- My flesh and my faith don't seem to get along.
- It's as though there were a Dr. Jekyll and Mr. Hyde on the inside. And it's gotten so bad that "the good that I would I do not and the evil which I would not that I do." To make matters worse, even when I would do good, evil is always present before me.

Because Paul suffered from these erratic and sudden shifts of personality, because there appears to be justifiable reason to support the view that Paul was possessed by some abnormal psycho-social traits—that's the basis for wanting to share with you today regarding this preacher predicament.

The time has come to take an honest look at preachers because sometimes we preachers are better at helping others than we are at helping ourselves . . . because sometimes our lives as preachers are in such a shambles that even when we have an opportunity to preach we have nothing whatsoever to say . . . because sometimes we can tell everybody else what well to draw from, but very often we have a hole in our own bucket. There is more than sufficient reason to suggest that there is a measure of psychosis in some of us, if not in all of us.

Now to be honest with Paul, and to be intellectually honest with you, it may not be possible to verify that Paul was clinically psychotic. I am aware of my limitations to make this diagnosis of Paul or any other preacher. Like Paul, I am a preacher and not a psychiatrist.

If, however, it is fair to say that one who is psychotic may be characterized by a deterioration of the normal intellectual and social functions, and if the psychotic may be said to have had a partial or complete withdrawal from reality and if the psychotic may be said to be one who is plagued by continuous worry or extreme behavior . . . .

If this is the criteria by which the psychotic is to be judged, then perhaps there is justifiable ground for this analysis of the psychosis in the preacher or, more particularly, this examination of the psychotic in the apostle Paul.

After all, Paul did tend to worry. He was always talking about "wrestling against principalities, against powers, against spiritual wickedness in high places." Paul *did* tend to worry. He sounds a little paranoid when he advises those who have just come to battle to "put on the whole armor of God."

If not psychotic, Paul is at least "shakey." After all, Paul does tend to teeter-totter somewhere on the edge of reality. It seems a little strange for a man to confess that he can't decide between living and dying. Paul never seems to be able to decide whether it is better to be absent from the body or present with the Lord.

Perhaps Paul is psychotic. And I'll be honest with you, I can't be sure about this, but I have a suspicion that what Paul may be suffering from is really a kind of classic schizophrenia.

Look at the rapid movements of his moods, the shifts of his personality. On one day he assures us of his calling and on the next he complains that he is least of all and not worthy to be called an apostle.

There's something wrong here. Anytime a man says: "The good that I would I do not; but the evil which I would not, that I do," something is wrong. Something is wrong with anybody that lives in that kind of unstable, vacillating, see-saw, on-again-off-again, hot-and-cold, topsy-turvy world.

I am haunted by this question of the psychotic in preachers. What is it about Paul, what is it about preachers, what is it about this preaching business that creates this psychosis factor? Of the causes which come rapidly to the surface of the mind the first may be *what Paul himself called "the foolishness of preaching."*

You do recall (1 Corinthians 1:21) that Paul suggested that, in fact, "it pleased God by the foolishness of preaching to save them that believe." Oh, the irony of it all! A preacher stands to preach and before he ever says a word he knows that he's engaged in *foolishness*.

- Preaching—Sunday after Sunday—and it's foolishness.
- Preaching—week after week—and it's foolishness.
- Preaching—folk forget what you said five minutes after the benediction: foolishness.
- Preaching—trying in a few minutes to undo the wrong folk have done in a lifetime: foolishness.
- Preaching—not so much because you want to but because you can't help it: foolishness.

Yes, it is foolishness. Paul knew it was foolishness. And yet, this same Paul was fond of saying: "Woe be unto me if I preach not the gospel."

This same Paul said men cannot hear without a preacher.

This same Paul wrote his son, Timothy, and told him in no uncertain terms: "Timothy, preach the Word, in season and out."

Perhaps the preacher is psychotic because of the nature of his calling and because of the sheer foolishness of preaching.

Yet again, the preacher may be psychotic or schizoid or on a mental roller coaster because he is so busy dealing with others that he has no time to deal with himself. I don't know how you feel about it, but it makes me shudder everytime I realize that when judgment comes, judgment will begin in the house of God. Even more to the point, judgment won't start in the pews; it will begin in the pulpit. This may be a strange excuse for preaching, but we are left only to conclude that

EVEN THE PREACHER NEEDS TO BE SAVED!

Preachers go to hell just like everybody else. Even preachers with academic degrees and long robes and television ministries must occasionally be reminded that "with the heart man believeth and with the mouth confession is made unto salvation." We are not exempt. Even preachers need to know that God's plan of salvation includes us too.

Don't you find what I am suggesting here strange? The world is on fire and on its way to hell, and preachers need to be saved. Honestly, I don't want to be so busy being pastor that I forget that I have a heaven to gain and a hell to shun. I don't want to be so busy being "Doctor This" or "Reverend That"

that I forget that one day I've got to stand in the judgment. I don't want to forget that soon and very soon, in the words of an old meter hymn:

> That awful day will surely come,
> The appointed hour make haste,
> When I must stand before the judge
> And stand the solemn test.

I don't want to be so busy "being in charge of being in charge," presiding over "committees on the committees," that I forget that like Nicodemus I too must be "born again." Paul says that the preacher always runs the danger that when he has preached to others, he himself should become a castaway.

The third factor which argues for the possibility of a psychotic preacher may be that *a change of name does not always indicate a change of nature.* You see, Paul's problem was that even though he was a preacher, sin kept on cropping up in his life. Now you must not forget that Paul's name at one time was Saul.

You do remember that Damascus Road experience?

You do remember that Saul was on his way down to Damascus in search of those who were followers after the way?

I know you remember how the Lord laid his hands on Saul. The Lord stepped into Saul's life in a way that picked him up and turned him around.

Consequently, there is no doubt in my mind that Saul was converted. Saul was as changed as any man can change. Saul was regenerated. Saul was sanctified. Saul was Holy Ghost—filled. No matter how one views Saul's experience, Saul was born again. As a result of this conversion experience, Saul's name was changed to Paul.

- Saul was the old man; Paul was the new man.
- Saul was possessed by that old nature; Paul had a new nature.
- Saul was carnal; Paul was spiritual.
- Saul died and Paul sprang to life.

But every once in a while that old Saul would show up in the new Paul.

That's it! That's my problem. That's your problem.

Yes, you've been saved, you've been born again, you've been converted. But every once in a while that old you shows up. You thought you were through with that old you, but he keeps on showing up. You joined church, got baptized, joined the choir, usher at the door, but every now and then that old you comes back to call. That's the problem. You know what you used to be and what folk used to call you. But now they call you "Reverend." Now they call you "Evangelist." Now they call you "Elder." Now they call you "Bishop." But you know the real story.

You changed your name, but somehow you didn't change your nature.

Jacob got his named changed to Israel, but every now and then that lying, cheating, scheming, conniving Jacob would show up in Israel. And that's because changing your name does not change your nature.

Jesus changed *Simon* to *Peter* and told him, "Upon this rock I will build my church." But almost in the same breath Jesus said, "Get thee behind me, Satan," to the same Peter, because a change of name does not mean a change of nature.

If we are honest, each of us must confess that at some time or another we are all like Paul.

We all have this haunting duality of personality:
- Saved, but still beset by sin.
- Converted, but still caught in the cross-fire of iniquity.
- Born again, but still backsliding.
- Baptized, but still on a downward path!

We all have this Paul-problem:
- Saint one day, sinner the next.
- Holy on Sunday, unholy on Monday.
- Righteous this week, irreligious next week.
- Shouting this Sunday, won't say "Amen" next Sunday.
- Loving today, hateful tomorrow.
- Leaping yesterday, limping today.

There is a dichotomy between what we planned to be and what we somehow became.

There is an ambivalence between the ideal and the real.

There is a polarity between what God intended and how we turned out.

That's why you have such difficulty with sin in your life. This is the reason for the repulsion and attraction you feel toward preachers. This explains why so many love to hate preachers and hate to love preachers.

The principle is this: *the same thing you see in the preacher is the same thing you see in yourself!* That same humanity that's in the preacher is the same humanity that's in you. So the question becomes not just how to deal with the tragedy of a psychotic preacher but how to deal with the psychotic in you!

Why am I able to stand today . . .
- With all my weakness and my wickedness,
- With all my faults and my failures,
- With all my shortcomings and disappointments,
- With all my trials and tribulations,
- With all my sins and transgressions,
- With all my rights and my wrongs?

I'm able to stand today . . .
- Not because I'm righteous.
- Not because I'm holy.
- Not because I've kept his commands so well.

I stand today because . . .
- I know the Lord laid his hands on me.
- I know the Lord saved my soul.
- I know the Lord called my name and touched my mouth.

Despite what I am, despite what I may not be, I am God's man. He alone decides to use me in spite of me.

If there is a word here for preachers, it may very well be that you ought not to worry over those psychological traits you can't understand. Don't be overanxious if your lifestyle doesn't seem to balance with your beliefs. Just let God have his way. If you let him, he'll make you what he wants you to be.

Well, Paul, how do you resolve this inner turmoil and conflict? The evidence is rather incriminating. Nobody said it for you—you said it yourself. You know the law is spiritual and yet you are carnal, sold unto sin.

What about it, Paul?

- What you do, you don't want to do.
- What you don't want to do, you do.
- What you hate, you do.
- The good that you would, you do not, and that which you would not, that you do.
- And when you would do good, evil is always present in you.

That's psychotic! That's bizarre behavior! That's sick! What about it, Paul?

I hear Paul's response: Yes, you are right. Your diagnosis is appropriate. That's why, every once in a while when I think about *who* I am, I have to say, Oh!

When I think about *what* I am, I have to say, Oh!

When I think about what I have *become,* I have to say, Oh!

When I think about how the Lord uses me in spite of me, I have to say, Oh!

When I think about how far I've come and how far I have to go, the only thing I can say is, Oh!

OH, WRETCHED MAN THAT I AM, WHO SHALL . . .

Who shall, not *what* shall . . .

Who shall, not what church shall . . .

Who shall, not what denomination shall . . .

Who shall deliver me from the body of this death?

I thank God through Jesus . . .

- Jesus will deliver.
- Jesus will deliver me from me.
- Jesus will deliver me from the me I don't wish to be.

Jesus will remove the strain of the psychotic from my personality and give me the strength to be the me that he intended me to be.

Amazing grace shall always be my song of praise,
For it was grace that bought my liberty.
I don't know why my Savior came to love me so;
He looked beyond my fault and saw my need.

I shall forever lift mine eyes to Calvary
To view the cross where Jesus died for me.
How marvelous that grace that caught my falling soul!
He looked beyond my fault and saw me need.

EPILOGUE

Athens

Brother preacher!

You really took me to task on this one! My gracious, am I really as bad as all that? Are the preachers you know as bad as all that?

Well, Beecher, I am not at all sure that some of your rather strong statements about my mental stability are as well-founded as you seem to think they are. There is a measure of the personality of every preacher in the sermon he or she is called to preach. The problem is that we are unsure of the extent of that measure. I continually thank my God upon every remembrance of you, Beecher, even though you cause me to question whether I was writing of mankind in general or if I really wrote concerning myself and failed to realize how self-revealing these words would become with the passage of time.

I now realize why your letter this time was so short. With this sermon, my son, you have managed to aggravate me to no end. However, because of my love for you, I must also forgive you. If we were in one accord in our understanding at all times, Beecher, we would never be blessed to experience the joy of this forgiveness and thus the renewal of friendship. So perhaps I am a bit schizoid, and perhaps I do suffer from some (would you believe "mild"?) form of psychosis. I have learned, however, in whatever state I am therewith to be content. I count it all joy.

I don't know why you chose to preach from this text (I perceive that this is not the first time you have waxed eloquent from these passages!), nor am I certain if the analysis you have made of me may not have a measure of self-analysis as well, however I am certain of the motive in my writing to the Romans in the first place.

You see, Beecher, as an apostle called to preach, I was constantly ministering to the needs of the saints. Many of those upon whom I was counting deserted me and left me on my own in some dangerous and treacherous fields of ministry. Much like a physician in time of great disease and plague, one is often so involved in innoculating others that one fails to innoculate himself. Soon the physician becomes infected with the very disease he seeks to cure in others. Consequently, the physician becomes the patient. The clearest tragedy, however, is when those of us who are among the sick attempt to heal ourselves.

Beecher, we could not preach to others, we could not seek the health and healing of others, if we were not acquainted with the great physician. His healing practice extends beyond the body to the mind. He is physician. He is psychologist. He is psychiatrist.

We are not above sin, my son. We have not been immunized against weaknesses of mind and body. Nevertheless, we have the assurance that even as we suffer in his name so shall we also share in his joy. How well you know, Beecher, that the very nature of this painful and unpredictable calling causes the world to question our sanity and our mental stability. This holy stigma which has attached itself to us causes us, on more than one occasion, to act in ways which the world cannot understand. But we know that our walk is a walk of faith. Our walk requires that we traffic in those places where the sane would never go and where even angels sometimes would fear to tread.

The pay for preachers, my son, often comes in installments of misunderstanding. Even those who are closest to us do not understand us. More than once we will stand perplexed by our own behavior — failing to understand what moves us, what motivates us, or what can save us. I thank my God that he who calls and claims also protects and provides. The psychological terms by which we are called are not to be compared to the glory of the Name by which we shall be known when he shall appear.

Do not dismay, Beecher. All things yet work together for the good, for the benefit, of those who love God and who understand his calling as consonant with his purpose and his power. Yes, we have been set apart, but we have not been removed. We must wrestle with our humanity as well as with the misunderstanding and the maltreatment of those to whom we are called to minister. He has called us, and our justification by faith is in his hand. Remember John's advice: it does not appear to us just what we shall be. But God has determined that ultimately we shall be like him and, what's more, we shall see him face to face. Hallelujah! That's good news! That, my brother, is the gospel.

Keep praying; keep preaching!

Your paranoid brother,
Paul

9

CASE DISMISSED

PROLOGUE

Washington, D.C.

Dear Paul:

I have finally learned what it means to "pray without ceasing" and to "rejoice evermore." While waiting for your response to "The Tragedy of a Psychotic Preacher" I did pray without ceasing, uncertain as to how it would affect you and how it would affect our relationship. Much as an erring child might feel, I wondered if I would incur your wrath or if you would be as empathetic with my clumsy preaching style as I had hoped.

Thanks be to God, you did not judge me harshly. Indeed, you not only aided me in my understanding of the spiritual and psychological forces at work in me, but your epistle renewed my faith and my joy. Thanks be to God also for the partnership in the gospel which we have shared from the first day until now. Because of your gentle spirit, Paul, you have aided me in my journey from faith to faith—from the immature faith of my younger days to the maturity of the faith which I now know in these last days, and from the faith which was necessary because of the blindness of spiritual ignorance to the informed faith which now consumes me and which assures me to trust the coming of light even while standing in the midst of darkness.

I am really excited, my brother, about what I am sending you today. Not because it is anything <u>better</u>, but because there is so much of who I am tied up in it.

Paul, I need not convince you that preachers can be somewhat complicated personalities. Often the community we serve can only see the tip of the iceberg. How true it is that everyone who hears you preach or who reads your sermon becomes an instant analyst and presumes to know all you are thinking and saying. This really bothers me Paul, because all of this analysis indicates that one's hearers think that there must be a hidden agenda or a coded message that the preacher is holding back. Why must the message and the motive of the preacher always be held in such suspicion and under such tension? Is it so impossible that we are who we are, we are what we are, and over the vast preponderance of the time, we say what we mean? After all, we preachers are not <u>that</u> complicated. Ah, well, I suppose that is one of the prerogatives of the pew.

At any rate, I am excited about this new sermon because it lets you in on another side of me, Paul. You see, I have this (not too secret) desire to be an attorney at law. Not the Judaic law of which you must be thinking, but the civil law. I want to argue cases and defend clients in a court of law. I know a jury would be putty in my hands. This is not ego speaking, Paul, but I really know that I would be a great criminal lawyer. And that is why I think it not coincidental that God has brought me to a city where there are more lawyers per square inch than any other city of the world. Sometimes God's sense of humor is amazing.

I was headed down that path—toward becoming a lawyer—once. But then God stepped into my life in a powerful and peculiar way. He completely turned my life, my ambition, around and, as you know, I have been preaching since. My call to ministry was the greatest and most traumatic event I have ever known. It radically changed my life. I confess, Paul, it was not as dramatic as your experience on the road to Damascus, but then some of us get the point more quickly than others. (I couldn't resist that one!)

Do you suppose that there are other preachers who, like me, have some other secret vocational calling? Others who realize that there is no alternative to their ministry but who long to realize some other potential or talent in another field of endeavor? Is there a way to merge and to blend what one wants to be and what one must be? Is there any ground for my fear that in even looking to that other possible life I may be guilty of putting my hand to the plough and then looking back?

These are the sort of haunting, nagging questions with which I live daily. Who knows, maybe God can even gain glory from what I meant to be!

In any case, Paul, I am sending along my sermon entitled "Case Dismissed." The substance of this sermon was inspired by those magnificent opening lines of yours, "There is now therefore no condemnation!"

If ever there was a sentence which encapsulated the intent of the gospel this is it. In a sense, Paul, this sermon is not original with me. The courtroom setting—placed in eternity with God as the judge and Satan and Mercy as the attorneys for the prosecution and defense respectively—is a kind of folk story that has circulated among preachers longer than I have been alive. I have taken some liberties with the story and its interpretation, however, and with a little theatric and dramatic spice. (By the way, some of my members say I tend toward histrionics from time to time. An unjust evaluation, I assure you.) I have tried to make it come alive for the eye, the ear, and the mind.

The result is that this sermon is, in form at least, completely separate and apart from the rest. All of us need to take a view to see what the end will be. If the end of life is judgment and a sentence of wrath, then why not get off now? If, however, there is yet hope for pardon, for parole, for exoneration, then there is good reason for the journey.

Perhaps, Paul, through this dramatic/theatric exercise we can come to see something of the multiple dimensions of the God-man relationship. Francis Schaeffer has written that God is both personal and infinite. There is about him that which is personal, but at the same time, infinite. There is something about God that permits him to possess both power and love; both of these divine-human qualities permit him to hear our needs and to act in response.

It may well be, Paul, that this sermon is a fragile attempt to express these ideas. Yet I pray that through this medium, borne on the wings of courtroom drama, perhaps we will be permitted to catch a glimpse of things as they really are and as they shall be when time shall turn to eternity. We can see ourselves in the light of both judgment and grace. We can see God in power and in compassion. We can rest secure in the knowledge that God is God—and it's all right!

Grace and peace!
Beecher

Sermon: CASE DISMISSED

> There is therefore now no condemnation to them which are in Christ Jesus, who walk not after the flesh, but after the Spirit. For the law of the Spirit of life in Christ Jesus hath made me free from the law of sin and death (Romans 8:1 KJV).

> Therefore, there is now no condemnation for those who are in Christ Jesus, because through Christ Jesus the law of the Spirit of life set me free from the law of sin and death (Romans 8:1–2 NIV).

There is a court convened somewhere within the precincts of eternity where every man stands on trial.

There is a court where men are accused and tried and where life and eternal life are weighed in the balance.

- The trial is not long.
- The charges are correct.
- The evidence is clear.
- The witnesses cannot be shaken.
- The attorneys are capable.
- The jury is just.
- There is a court.

The rich and the poor, the educated and the ignorant, the cultured and the crude, they all must stand trial, one-by-one, in that place where the hidden comes to light, where secrets are shouted, and where the real is revealed.

- Who you are will not be important.
- Who or what you know will not count.
- Neither your good intentions nor your unfulfilled plans will be of any value.
- The saintliness of your mother and the godliness of your father will be of no avail.

There is a court.

You must stand trial there. You and I must stand there one day for ourselves.

There is a court convened somewhere in the precincts of eternity where everyone stands on trial.

Not only is there a court, but perhaps you ought to be acquainted with the Judge. The Judge of whom I speak presides over the court of eternity.

He always has been the Judge, because he was before the beginning, and he will be after the beginning is no longer able to begin.

This Judge of whom I speak is the Truth, and he cannot lie. He is the creator of the whole universe.

Nothing exists that was not shaped in his hands.

He can do what he wants to do because he already knows what he needs to know.

His court is extensive. He is Judge of all the earth.

He rules alone. He is Judge all by himself.

If you are not acquainted with this Judge of whom I speak the Hebrews called him *El*, the Deity, or *El Shaddai*, the Mountain, or *Adonai*, Lord or King, or *Yahweh*, Jehovah Lord, which means "to be" or "to be actively present."

If you still do not know this Judge of whom I speak, listen to what my forebears said:

> He's Alpha and Omega, the Beginning and the End,
> Fairest of ten thousand,
> Lily of the valley, bright and morning star.

He is omnipotent, omniscient, and omnipresent. They said—your parents and mine—they said he is:

> A walking cane and a leaning post,
> A comfort to the lonely,
> Bread to the hungry and water to the thirsty.

But above all else, as Isaiah has it, he is the Judge who sits above the circle of the earth. He is the Judge who measures out the waters in the hollow of his hand. He is the Judge who meted out the heavens with a span and comprehended the dust of the earth in a measure. He is the Judge who weighed the mountains in scales and the hills in a balance. And, besides all of that, I declare he is the Judge who sits high and looks low.

There is a Judge, I tell you, and there is a court covenened somewhere in the precincts of eternity where every man stands on trial.

Perhaps then . . . if it is true that there is a court and that man is on trial and that God himself sits as Judge . . . perhaps then it might be of interest to hear just a bit of what might go on in such a trial. If it is true that I must stand trial and if it is true that you also must stand before the solemn bar of the very judgment and justice of God, then perhaps you might be interested to hear what might go on when man stands on trial.

HEAR YE! HEAR YE! THE COURT OF ETERNITY IS NOW
IN SESSION. GOD ALMIGHTY, PRESIDING.

[I am looking and listening now by means of a sanctified imagination as God calls the court to order. I see that Satan is the attorney for the prosecution and Mercy is the attorney for the defense. Not only are the attorneys present but I hear God calling for the jury to be seated. Do you see them?

[Justification and Sanctification are seated side by side. Right and Righteousness have taken their seats with their arms folded in judgment. Faith, Hope, and Charity have come in, closely followed by Memory, Conscience, and Guilt. Goodness just entered the chambers, and the last one in was Justice, and he just closed the door.

[Let's listen in on the testimony!]

Transcript of Trial (Part 1)

Judge: Bailiff, read the charges against Man.

Bailiff: Your Honor, there are thirty-six charges held against Man according to the deposition filed by the apostle Paul.

The apostle Paul has charged Man in Romans 1:18 with ungodliness and unrighteousness; in Romans 1:25 of changing the truth of God into a lie; in Romans 1:29–30 of being filled with all unrighteousness, fornication, wickedness, covetousness, and maliciousness and of being guilty of envy, murder, debate, deceit, malignity, whispering, backbiting, hating God, pride, inventing evil, and disobedience.

Your Honor, Man is charged in Romans 2:5 of a hard and impenitent heart; in Romans 2:8 Man is charged with contentiousness and unwillingness to obey the truth; and in Romans 2:24 Man is charged not only with blasphemy, but with causing the name of God to be blasphemed.

If it please the court, Your Honor, Man is charged in Romans 3:10 of a failure to be righteous; and in Romans 3:13–18 the evidence reveals that Man has a throat that is an open sepulchre, with his tongue he has used deceit, the poison of asps is under his lips, his mouth is full of cursing and bitterness, his feet are

154

swift to shed blood, destruction and misery are in his way, and there is no fear of God in his eyes.

[We continue to listen in on the trial of Man as God speaks.]

Judge: Satan, are you ready with the argument for the prosecution?

Satan: I am, Your Honor.

Your Honor, I move for a summary judgment.

[The court is visibly stunned!]

I realize my motion is rather unusual considering the gravity of the case. But I also realize that no matter what the attorney for the defense might have to say, it will be so lacking in substance and judgment that perhaps we could save the court some time just by asking for summary judgment. Make no mistake about it, Your Honor, on every charge Man is guilty. Even Man knows that Man is guilty. There can be no alibi, no alternative pleading, no counterclaim or cross-claim. The evidence is not circumstantial. In point of fact, the evidence is *prima facie*. Man's guilt is obvious on its face. Your Honor, I move for summary judgment.

[We now see Mercy moving to his feet, and the tension mounts in the courtroom as Mercy makes his opening statement.]

Mercy: Your Honor, I object to the motion of the prosecution. All we've heard so far are a lot of general claims. All we've heard so far are allegations which, as yet, have been unsubstantiated by any evidence introduced into this court of divine law. All we've heard so far, Your Honor, are rumors and allegations, and the prosecution has not offered up one witness in support of his claims. There is no preponderance of evidence. Man is on trial here for his eternal life and he's entitled to a trial. There is no value in a summary judgment at this point.

Judge: Objection sustained! Attorney Satan, call your first witness.

Satan: Your Honor, rather than call my first witness, if it please the court, since the learned counsel for the defense is so concerned about evidence, I want to enter into evidence this book called the Holy Bible. As you know, Your Honor, since it's your book, there are 66 books in the Bible. There are 929 chapters in the Old Testament and 260 chapters in the New Testament, and it runs from Genesis to Revelation.

But if it please the court, I want to enter into evidence this Book of Books, this book of the Lord's Prayer and the Shepherd's Psalm, this book of the fruit of the Spirit and the Golden Rule. In this book it says that . . .

Adam and Eve were deceitful and disobedient;
Abraham was a liar;
Noah was a drunkard;
Isaac was not to be trusted;
Jacob was a trickster;
Moses was a murderer;
Jeremiah was a crybaby;
Samson was a playboy;
Solomon was a philanderer;
David couldn't tend to his own sheep without stealing another's lamb;
Peter had foot-in-mouth disease;
Thomas was a coward;
Judas was a thief.

And that's why there is no doubt in my mind that the charges are clear and the guilt is without question. There is no longer any reason to prolong the proceedings. Man is guilty, and the Book—Your Book—is here to prove it.

Interlude

In case you have wearied of these legal proceedings, let me assure you that you are more than spectators in this trial. If Man is on trial, you are on trial. If mankind in general has been accused, then—because you are flesh and blood, because you were designed with dust and framed with flesh, because you have to live confined within these temporary and decaying houses we call bodies—you, specifically you, have been accused as well. The charges are not general and vague; they will not be applied to a nameless somebody or anybody. The charges are specific and personal and pointed directly at you. Don't look now, but the indictment is your indictment.

As you look at the long list of charges against you, permit me to remind you of your rights:

> You have the right to remain silent. Anything you say can and will be used as evidence against you in a court of law. You have the right to an attorney and if you want an attorney and cannot afford one, an attorney will be appointed without cost to you. Do you understand?

Don't speak up now. You have the right to remain silent.

Don't try to defend yourself. He who defends himself has a fool for an attorney.

You have the right to remain silent. The charges are serious. There's only a step between you and eternal death and eternal damnation.

You have the right to remain silent. It's hard to explain away sin. The more you talk, the deeper your distress.

You have the right to remain silent. Anything you say will be used against you.

In other words, the words you use to defend yourself will be the very words that will be used in your prosecution. Don't try to explain your sin. Don't try to justify your sin. You have the right to remain silent.

While examining the case against mankind, I've discovered another reason to remain silent: *We don't have the law on our side either!* In fact, as I've reviewed this legal brief that Paul has designed against mankind, Paul says that the problem he faced and the problem we face is caused by the law. Paul says that the law defined sin. Paul says, "I wouldn't have known what sin was were it not for the law." Paul says he was in search of a spiritual law but somehow he got caught up in a carnal law. And somehow the very law that was supposed to bring life brought death. Paul says he was anxious to cooperate with the law of God, but instead he got tangled up with another law that was in his members that in fact brought him to a deeper sense of captivity and a deeper sense of sin.

And so, the implication of Paul's comment is that the law cannot save you. Follow every law in the first five books of the Law, and you will discover that the law cannot save you. Follow the Ten Commandments to the letter and you will discover that the Ten Commandments alone cannot save you. Become a religious Pharisee and follow all the laws that are underneath the law. But it won't save you. Become a spiritual elitist where there has never been and never will be anybody as spiritual and as "in the word" as you are, and it still won't save you. Learn all the hymns in the hymn book and quote all the Scripture that you please, but it still won't save you.

Follow closely, if you please. Let's listen again to the testimony in the case.

Transcript of Trial (Part 2)

> *Judge:* Attorney Mercy, please call your first witness.
>
> *Mercy:* If it please the court, Your Honor, I don't have any witnesses to call. I don't have anything to enter into evidence. In fact I told my client that there was only one way to come to court.
>
> *Judge:* Then how does Man come before this court?
>
> *Man:* "Just as I am without one plea."
>
> *Mercy:* If it please the court, the defense rests.
> No plea bargain, we rest our case.

No long arguments about due process, we rest our case.

No tactics of delay or courtroom drama, we rest our case.

No surprise witnesses, no detailed defense, we rest our case.

If you accuse Man of being an accessory to sin, in some way aiding and contributing to sin, without objection we rest our case.

If you accuse Man of being an accomplice to sin, engaging with others in the commission of sin, without objection we rest our case.

If you accuse Man of being culpable of sin, deserving moral blame, more at fault than at guilt, without objection we rest our case.

[The courtroom is still astir with this surprise move on the part of the attorney for the defense. The jurors have retired to deliberate, but it appears that they are already returning to their seats.

[Justice is the foreman of the jury, and we see him stand as God, the Judge, speaks.]

Judge: Members of the jury, have you reached a verdict about Man?

Justice: Yes, Your Honor. We the members of the jury find the defendant guilty as charged on all counts.

Summation

And that's your case and my case. If you could look back over a summary of your sins from the day of your birth till now, you'd have to admit: Guilty as charged.

You name it, we've done it: Guilty as charged.

Doing things our way rather than God's way: Guilty as charged.

Secret sins and closet conduct: Guilty as charged.

Charged by sin, arrested by justice, and convicted by guilt: Guilty as charged.

Taking God for granted: Guilty as charged.

Receiving God's blessings, but failing to thank him: Guilty as charged.

Living on land we don't own, living in houses we did not build, eating food we did not plant, yet refusing to give him a dime out of a dollar: Guilty as charged.

> *Judge:* Would the attorneys for the prosecution and the defense please approach the bench?

It appears that now the Judge is asking for a pre-sentencing report. The Judge wants to be sure that the punishment fits the crime. All the options will be explored to be certain that there is justice in God's judgment. The question of the pre-sentencing report is, did the defendant have a chance?

Did somebody warn Man of the error of his ways?

Perhaps if Man did not know, as through ignorance of the law or some other extenuating circumstances, there would be reason for leniency or a reason for the judgment to be less severe that it might ordinarily be.

But the pre-sentencing report reveals that Man did know.

- Moses gave man the law.
- The dispensation of promise gave man a way out and a way up.
- The era of the Judges gave man an opportunity for human government.
- Isaiah, Jeremiah, and Ezekiel ushered in the age of prophecy.
- Matthew, Mark, Luke, and John gave man the gospel.
- Teachers have been teaching. Preachers have been preaching. Singers have been singing.

Man has had the Bible for his treasure, the church for worship, the Sunday school for instruction; and the Judge himself sent Jesus in a dispensation of grace. Man is just as guilty as sin, and the sentence is ultimately left in the hand and the heart of the Judge.

But now it's God's option. The case is closed. The verdict

has been given. The jury's work is done. Let's listen to the summation and the sentencing by the Judge.

The Sentence

Judge: The jury's work is done. In the eyes of God and in the eyes of the law, Man is guilty as charged. Attorney Satan has proven his case beyond a shadow of a doubt. The Bible does say that Man is a sinner. But that same Bible says: "Though your sins be as scarlet, they shall be as white as snow; though they be red like crimson, they shall be as wool."

That same Bible says: "There is therefore now no condemnation to them which are in Christ Jesus."

Therefore my sentence is: CASE DISMISSED!

While I recognize there is no precedent for this strange judgment of the bench, you need to be aware that while the jury was out I sent Jesus.

I sent Jesus down through forty-and-two generations.
I sent Jesus down to Jordan's stream.
I sent Jesus to heal the sick and raise the dead.
I sent Jesus to walk on water and calm the sea.
I sent Jesus to turn water into wine and divide loaves of bread.
I sent Jesus to stir water at Bethesda pool and to touch the eyes of the man born blind.
I sent Jesus to dark Gethsemane.
I sent Jesus to Pilate's judgment hall and Caiaphas' courthouse.
I sent Jesus to a hill far away and to an old rugged cross.

[The Judge pauses to take a drink of water, and the courtroom remains in awesome silence until he resumes his statement.]

Jesus died so I could tell you: Case dismissed.
Jesus died so that Man might live.
Jesus died so that Adam could get back to the east gate of Eden.
Jesus died so that Noah would give up his wine.

161

Jesus died so that Isaac's life could be spared.

Jesus died so that Jeremiah could dry his tears.

Jesus died so that Samson could find his strength.

Jesus died so that Solomon would know the source of wisdom.

Jesus died so that David would know goodness and mercy.

Jesus died so that Mary would have a testimony.

Jesus died so that Thomas could feel the print of the nail.

Jesus died so that the thief could hear him say: "This day shalt thou be with me in paradise."

Case dismissed!

EPILOGUE

Tarsus

My beloved Beecher:

I suppose the tears will soon end their flow.

I have been strangely moved. But not by your sermon-drama, which I would call "theological theatrics"!

It was something else that gave me problems, Beecher. It is more than I can bear to hear of an attorney called Satan. You give him far too much credit. Putting the Bible on the witness stand — an immortal book before an imaginary jury — strains the mind, to say the least. (I suppose this, too, falls under the category of your "sanctified imagination"? One day we shall discuss this, young man!) I have to ask you whether this kind of sermonizing-evangelizing really does what you seem to think it is designed to do. Is the consequence of this sermon that souls are saved or sinners entertained?

But something else bothers me more, Beecher, something intensely personal. You see, trials are not abstract for me. I know the pain and trauma of standing trial. I know personally the anxiety one can experience when life is being weighed in the balance. Evidently you have not had this experience or else you would know the heavy weight one feels when spectators have gathered to see your public humiliation. The witness stand is no place for cowards, my son. I sense that you twentieth-century Christians have never had to testify for him except in the safety of your sanctuaries. Try testifying when your neck is at stake.

Beecher, have you met your Felix, have you met your Agrippa? With the judgment of God I know there is at least the possibility of grace. With the judgment of man there can only be imprisonment, sickness, and death.

These are weighty matters, my son. The business of standing trial for one's sins and shortcomings is a thought that is often delayed for the reality of standing trial for preaching Christ and him crucified. I know you did not mean to gain this response from me, but try writing this sermon again after you've "been there!"

I am strangely moved. You have caused me to remember what real trials are really like. I suppose the tears will soon end their flow.

> *Your brother in Christ,*
> *Paul*

P.S.: God has granted your desire. You simply plead your case in a higher court!

10

THE POWER
OF THE POTTER

PROLOGUE

Washington, D.C.

Dear Paul:

Here I am again. It's nearly midnight. Sunday will be here in a second, and I still don't have the first thing to say in the morning.

Sometimes this is really torture—this sermon-writing business. I really wish I was one of those preachers—you know, the glib ones, the ones with a pithy quotation that fits every subject, complete with photographic memories, who never use a manuscript or notes—who seem to have no trouble coming up with a challenging sermon every Sunday and who preach with such grace and ease? Why does this weekly session have to be so full of anxiety and fear for me. After all these years you'd think I'd have learned by now.

You know what's really funny, Paul? Here I am in a library surrounded by books; I have books on theology, books on church history, books on homiletics. I even have the sermons of preachers from more generations than I can count, and I still find it hard to put together a decent sermon to preach. There oughta be a law. I even have a file of my own sermons, and they don't help either. Somehow sermons seem to lose their flavor; they grow stale. (Or is it that they lose their relevance and no longer suit the context for this new day of preaching?) The challenge we modern-day preachers face, Paul, is the challenge of remaining fresh and meaningful and relevant. The trouble is that at midnight on Saturday night, it's mighty hard to worry about being relevant!

Don't misunderstand me. I've been working on this sermon a long time. I've been reading the thoughts of others and meditating and praying over what God would say through this word, but there must be a clog in the vessel preventing that word from coming through. Do you have that problem, Paul?

Sometimes I find that if I can say aloud to myself what I am trying to say in the sermon to others, it helps me to verbalize my thoughts and then the writing comes more easily. Are you ready to listen?

One of the things that really disturbs me about God is that I don't know what he's trying to make out of me. It doesn't take me long to realize that God has some purpose for my life or I wouldn't be here. And yet when I realize that my life fails to measure up to the expectations that I believe he has of me, then I wonder what it is that God really had in mind when he brought me into being.

Let's take the thought a step further. One of the things that really disturbs me about God is that I don't know what he's trying to make out of us. By us I mean the people of black skin whom he has brought into this world and then put in places of bigotry and racism. I realize that suffering produces patience and character and hope and the rest, but enough is enough already. How long must black people suffer human indignity before God moves his hand? How long must our brothers and sisters in South Africa suffer the ravages of apartheid before God calls a halt? How many lives must be lost in the countries of the Third World because of starvation and malnutrition and disease before that which is divine moves again in the realm of the human? What is God doing to us? To what end? It seems as though something is always standing in the way of right, of good. Is it God?

Paul, you haven't helped with my question. If God has made me as I am, do you mean that I don't have the right to ask him why? Is that what you meant when you asked rhetorically if the Potter has power over the clay? Certainly the Potter has power over the clay, but does not the Potter have an obligation to be responsible and compassionate in terms of what he does with the clay?

You certainly haven't helped at all when you go on to assert that the Potter also makes some vessels to honor and other vessels unto dishonor. Is this an arbitrary action? Is this a premeditated action? Does God himself participate in our suffering by designing the suffering and by becoming the architect of human agony? Are we not all God's children? Are we not all created equal? Surely God does not really participate and condone this kind of inequity? What kind of God would he be if he did?

All these questions! Is it any wonder I am disturbed! I know the standard answers, the pat philosophical phrases, and the trite theological expressions, but somehow their taste is offensive in my mouth. I am more than an inanimate object; a vessel, but more than a vessel. I am human. And I really don't know what God is trying to make out of me. Does he?

Help, it's too late to wrestle any more. I'm tired and I want to go to bed. . . .

It's 3 A.M. and I'm finally through. Or maybe it's through with me. In any case, it's all I've got. I'm anxious to hear from you, soon.

> Your new son in the gospel,
> Beecher

Sermon: THE POWER OF THE POTTER

O man, who art thou that repliest against God? Shall the thing formed say to him that formed it, Why hast thou made me thus? Hath not the potter power over the clay, of the same lump to make one vessel unto honor, and another unto dishonor? (Romans 9:20–21).

The purpose of this time of our sharing together is at once transparent and patently clear. It is to affirm that God himself molds us and makes us and holds us in his hands. I am aware, of course, that for the mature Christian this affirmation is not new; it does not break new theological or philosophical ground. Additionally, I am aware that for those who are veteran soldiers of the cross, this word which speaks of God's intervention into human affairs is not necessarily a word of fresh revelation. On the other hand, for those who may be interested not only in *who* God is but *what* God does and *why* God does it, it will be important to remember that what I really seek to affirm is that God himself molds us and makes us and holds us in his hands.

Perhaps you have not considered the hands of God. Perhaps you have given little attention to the importance or the purpose of the hands of God.

- God's hands are symbolic of his compassion as well as of his power.
- God's hands are indicative of his involvement in human affairs.
- God's hands are parabolic of his possessiveness and of his strength.
- God's hands are a paradigm of his presence as well as of his protection.
- God's hands are representative of his action as well as of his authority and his autonomy.

In other words . . .

God upholds us with his hands.

God shelters us in the deep places of the earth in his hands.

God protects the sheep of his pasture and he holds them in his hands.

God scoops out valleys and molds mountains.

God holds the universe in a balance of his beneficence, keeps nature in harmony with the holy, and measures the whole of the cosmos by the plumbline of his justice and his judgment—and he does all that in his hands.

David suggested that even if you take the wings of the morning and dwell in the uttermost parts of the sea, even there his hand will lead you and his right hand will hold you.

Ezekiel discovered that when the hand of the Lord was upon him he developed a strange and unique preaching power that enabled even dry bones to hear the word of the Lord.

There is something strange about his hands. Even Jesus, as he hung dying on Calvary's tree, was heard to proclaim "Father, into thy hands I commend my spirit."

It would do well for you to consider the hands of God, for whether you know it or not, God himself molds us and makes us and holds us in his hands.

This discussion of the use God makes with his hands was prompted, in the main, by a rather disturbing passage of Scripture found here in the eighth chapter of Paul's epistle to the Roman community of Christians. Paul had come so far— beginning with his insistence on the power of the proclaimed word and soaring to new heights in his argument on just- ification by faith and then, at last, to come to that final valedictory of confidence and faith: nothing "shall be able to separate us from the love of God, which is in Christ Jesus our Lord."

Now, however, this exuberant and exultant Paul is a rather mournful and melancholy Paul. There is something sad and forlorn about this word of Paul's, this interrogative of a Tarsus preacher:

> *Hath not the potter power over the clay,*
> *of the same lump*
> *to make one vessel unto honor and another unto dishonor?*

Suddenly it appears that there is a nameless, faceless someone with whom Paul is holding conversation. The essence of this conversation is that the one to whom Paul is speaking has suggested that

GOD IS NOT FAIR!

After all, what kind of God is this that is so biased that he prefers some and ignores others?

What kind of God is this that is so discriminatory that he exalts some and brings others low?

What kind of God is this that is so pejorative that some have and others have not?

God is not fair.

In the first instance the argument is put forward that God is not fair because *God has not kept his promise*. God chose Israel through the process of divine adoption; God showed Israel his glory in the cleft of a rock; God protected Israel with cloud by day, fire by night, and manna on the ground; God gave Israel his covenant and his law; God could be found in temple worship and in Israel's patriarchs. God promised that of all nations *Israel* would be blessed. But now it looks like God does not keep his promise.

Paul is now preaching to Gentiles who are not Jews by birth. There are those now who are claiming the promise who are not the natural offspring of Abraham. They are no longer talking about the children of Abraham but they are talking about the children of the promise, and they say if somebody is getting something that we are not getting, if somebody is getting something that only we are supposed to get that means that God has not kept his promise and, more than that, it means that God is not fair.

But that's not the only way that God is not fair. God is not fair because he obviously is biased and discriminates against his children. God violates the basic tenets of human rights when he fails to give to the one that should have and gives abundantly to the one who should not have.

You see, Jacob and Esau had the same father. Yes, they were twins, but Esau was born first and, as a consequence,

Esau should have received the blessing and the inheritance of the father. But in point of fact *before*—how unfair can you get?—before they were born God said, "The older shall serve the younger." Not only that, God is so unfair that he let it be known that "Jacob have I loved, but Esau have I hated."

God is unfair. All you have to do is read the Scripture and you will see how unfair God is. There the children of Israel were in bondage in Egypt. There they were, oppressed by hard and cruel task masters. A new Pharaoh had arisen in Egypt that knew not Joseph. As a result, they worked from sunup to sundown making brick without straw and mortar without clay. Not only that but this Book says that God raised up Pharaoh and then hardened his heart. It looked as if Pharaoh had a hard enough heart on his own, but then God got in it and hardened Pharaoh's heart even more. And then when somebody said, "God, why did you do that?" or when somebody asked, "God, what did you have in mind when you treated us like that?" or when somebody raised the inquiry, "God, what is your plan or your purpose or your priority?" God simply said: "I will have mercy on whom I have mercy, and I will have compassion on whom I have compassion." And that's why this one against whom Paul argues, this one against whom Paul rails, this one toward whom Paul directs his sermonic diatribe, suggests to Paul, "Paul, *God is not fair!*"

This whole matter, then, of the unfairness of God, seems to speak a relevant and resonant word to our age. For, it seems to me, that there are some among us who would join in the accusation that God is not fair.

When life turns us upside down and inside out, it looks as if God has not kept his promise.

When our burdens press us down and when our burdens become too heavy to bear, somebody wants to know, "God, what have you done for me lately?"

When your bedroom becomes a sickroom and you remember that God promised to be a doctor that has never lost a patient, that's when you want to know, "Where are you, God, when I need you?"

When it looks like life is about to leave our bodies and we

have not yet reached three score and ten, sometimes it looks like God has not kept his promise.

Strangely enough, this word applies to those who love the Lord. Maybe I ought to remind you that just because you love the Lord does not mean that you won't have hard trials.

Just because you've joined the church does not mean that you're going to live your life on "flowery beds of ease."

Just because you've been born again and you've given your life to the Lord does not mean that you won't have enemies on every hand; it does not mean that the hounds of hell won't be on your trail. And when you go to church and you give your tithes and offerings and you serve and give your time and your talent and you still don't seem to be any better in the church than you were in the world, that's the time when it looks like God is unfair.

What really makes it seems as though God is unfair, however, is when the rascals of the world have everything and you don't have anything. Just look at Jacob.

- Jacob whose name means "supplanter" or "one who follows after."
- Jacob—selfish, crafty, deceitful, deceptive, liar, thief, cheat, fraud.

Jacob was all this and more, yet Jacob got the blessing over Esau! There are a whole lot of folk who don't ever do any good and yet they get the blessing. That's not fair. There are a whole lot of folk who just force their way in front of you when you are in line for the blessing and they get it and you don't. That's not fair. While you are trying to be a Christian and trying to love everybody and trying to make sure you say the right things and bringing your tithes and offerings to the storehouse, there is somebody else who is stepping over people and stepping on people, and they are the ones who drive the big cars, dress in the finest clothes, live in the most fabulous homes, and always have a wad of money, and you can't pay your bills or meet next month's rent. It's not fair.

Look yet again and you will discover that the thing which really makes it appear that God is not fair is when all the evidence seems to indicate that God is himself involved in the crime. You see, when the unfairness of God surfaces in some soul, it will not be long before some preacher comes to remind you that God knows all, God sees all, and God hears all.

It will not be long before some trumpeter of the gospel will declare that there is nothing that has happened or that is happening or that will happen which is not already in the will and in the mind and in the heart of God. It will not be long before some contemporary prophet will come insisting that there is nothing beyond the gaze of God and that all of the circumstances of life are but a part of the perfect plan for his people.

If that be the case, however, then God himself is a part of the problem. If we are sinners and God knows our circumstance, how can God find fault? If the events of our lives are a part of God's will, then how can God judge those who have not resisted that will? If God structures all things according to his will and if his will is being done, then religion is a hoax because there is then nothing that we can do to alter our condition or to change our fortune. And if that is the case, then it is abundantly true that God is not fair.

And so I wanted to share this as the theological, philosophical argument; I wanted to share this as the hermeneutic backdrop for Paul's response to his nameless and faceless redactor. For here, Paul, in the presence of this elaborate and persuasive and convincing argument for the unfairness of God, rather calmly replies:

> Nay but, O man, who art thou
>   that repliest against God?
> Shall the thing formed
>   say to him that formed it,
> Why hast thou made me thus?
> Hath not the potter
>   power over the clay?

What is Paul really saying here? First of all, I'm led of the Holy Spirit to tell you that I believe there is more than an implication in Paul's thinking that *it is dangerous to want God to be fair!*

Tell me . . .

- If God is fair, how soon must we face our transgressions in the light of day?
- If God is fair, how soon shall we see our secret sins cast in the light of his countenance?
- If God is fair, how soon shall we hear what goes on in the dark shouted from the rooftops?
- If God is fair, how soon shall he remind us of promises we have made and have not kept?
- If God is fair, how soon shall he remind us of those times he preferred us over others and we have not been grateful enough to say "thank you"?

If God is fair, says Zechariah, tell me who may abide the day of his coming?

It's a dangerous thing to want God to be fair. The old folk used to say, "If justice plumbed the line, we would have been gone long ago." It may not be wise to look for the fairness of God, after all. We may be better off looking for the mercy of God.

The second implication here is that not only is it dangerous to want God to be fair, but it is also *dangerous to want to argue with God*. I detect a little sarcasm in Paul's voice when he asks, "Who are you that you want to argue with God?"

- Who are you? Made out of dust and spit.
- Who are you? Made lower than angels.
- Who are you? Conceived in sin and shapen in iniquity.
- Who are you? Your ways are not his ways and your thoughts are not his thoughts.
- Who are you? You live in a land for which you did not labor; you live in cities which you did not build; you drink from vineyards that you did not plant.

Who are you? It's dangerous to want to argue with God.

The biblical record reveals that Job tried to argue with God one day. When Job looked at his dwindling assets and his mounting liabilities, Job wanted to argue with God. When Job looked and discovered that because of God he had lost his children and his servants, his wife and his home, Job wanted to argue with God. When it finally dawned on Job that his castle had become an ash pile and his regal garments had become sackcloth, and when he looked with horror into his mirror and saw the grotesque and deformed body that he could not recognize as his own and, indeed, could hardly imagine a body so covered with boils from the crown of his head to the sole of his feet, Job wanted to argue with God. When Job heard the bride of his youth, the mother of his children, the love of his life, counsel him to curse God and die, Job wanted to argue with God. Job said: "Oh that I knew where I might find him! that I might come even to his seat! I would order my cause before him, and fill my mouth with arguments."

But God's response was, "Job, I'll argue with you, but first there's a question I want to ask you:

"Where were you when I laid the foundation of the earth?

"You're so smart.

"Where were you when I laid the measure or stretched the line upon it?

"You've got so many questions.

"Where were you when I fastened the foundations and when I laid the cornerstone?

"You think I'm so unfair.

"Where were you when I shut up the sea with doors, made a garment out of the clouds, and made a swaddling band with thick darkness?

"You're so inquisitive about what I'm doing.

"Where were you when the morning stars sang together and when the sons of God shouted for joy?"

The third implication is that *God is able to use those events we do not understand and to use those persons who do not know him.*

Let me see if I can make this plain. You see, there are some events in my life that I would rather not have. There are some events in my life that are uncomfortable and which appear to be unprofitable and, if I had my way, I would avoid those events and circumstances altogether. But somehow God is able to take those events I do not understand and put a lesson in my life that otherwise would not be there.

- Pharaoh and his horses taught Moses how to use what was already in his hand.
- War and the jealousy of Saul taught David how to walk through the valley and the shadow of death.
- Starvation and the imminence of death taught Elijah that God had somebody beside him.
- Sickness and a fifteen-year diagnosis taught Hezekiah the value of a day.
- Darius and his lions' den taught Daniel how to pray.
- Nebuchadnezzar and his fiery furnace taught three Hebrews boys that no matter how mean the opposition may be, God is still able.

But God does not just teach his lessons with events. God teaches lessons by persons. You see . . .
- It's our enemies who teach us how to pray.
- It's our adversaries that teach us how to trust.
- It's our foes that give us faith.

Look closely here! Paul said that the potter has power over the clay. In fact, when we began this sermonic journey, all I wanted to affirm was that God molds us and makes us and holds us in his hand. It's no news to you that every potter has the job of molding and making and holding. However, I even realize that Paul has a philosophical problem with his argument because, after all, man is not a pot. Paul has a philosophical problem here, I tell you. Because if man is simply a lump of clay then man has no responsibility for what he does or does not do.

But these philosophical arguments aside, the reasons that God is involved in the pottery process is that God needs instruments and not objects. Any potter can make an object to sit on the shelf. Any potter can make an artifact that is a thing of beauty and a joy forever. Any potter can make an item of retail sale that men can purchase or leave alone. But God does not need objects, God needs instruments. Far too many who are engaged in the Christian enterprise are objects, but they're not instruments.
- An instrument says I'm good for something.
- An instrument says I have purpose.

- An instrument says I have value.
- An instrument says I can be used.

The goal of this Christian journey is for God to be able to use us.

I want him to use me.

- I may not always understand how or why, but use me.
- Others may have what I ought to have, but use me.
- I may have trials and tribulations, but use me.
- Friends may not understand why I serve him, but use me.
- Some may laugh because I struggle and strain, but use me.

> Use me, Lord, use me for thy service.
> Use me, Lord, help me tell thy story.
> Oh, use me, Lord
> Use me, oh Lord, I pray!

Always remember that the potter does have power over the clay. The potter has creative power. He brings into being that which was not.

The potter has creative power. He can take nothing and make something out of it.

The potter has creative power. He fashions the form in his mind and then brings it to pass simply by the moving of his hands.

The potter has creative power. He can stoop down in the dust of the earth and pick up lumps of clay and breathe the breath of life into it until it walks and talks like a natural man. The potter has creative power.

But more, the potter has re-creative power. Jeremiah says that sometimes the vessel is spoiled in the potter's hand. Sometimes the vessel does not do what it was designed to do. But the potter just takes it and breaks it and molds it and makes it what he would have it to be. I'm glad to know that when I'm spoiled and broken, the Lord is not through with me yet. I want him to re-create me.

I know the potter has power, and I want him to have power over me.

- Power over my life.
- Power over my feet.
- Power over my eyes.
- Power over my heart.
- Power over my head.
- Power over my home.
- Power over my job.
- Power over my church.
- Power. Wonder-working power.

We end where we began: God molds us and makes us and holds us in his hand. No matter what happens in this life, I'm in his hand. What a mighty God we serve! Right or wrong, up or down, poverty or wealth, sickness or health, come what may, I am in his hand. Hallelujah, I am in his hand.

It's all in his hands. It's all in his hands,
Whatever the problem may be.
It's all in his hands. It's all in his hands.
If you let him, he'll fix it for you!

EPILOGUE

Jerusalem

Dear Beecher:

Grace, mercy, and peace from God the Father and his Son, our Savior, the Lord Jesus Christ, to whom be honor, and glory and dominion forever. Amen.

Beecher, your tendency toward midnight writing must be contagious. If you are unable to read my script, it is because the candlelight by which I write makes it difficult if not impossible to do so. Jerusalem is a beautiful city at night. The flicker of flames along the pathways gives to this city of David an etherial glow. As I view it from the lattice of my window I can see across the Kedron Valley to the Mount of Olives on one

177

side, and just below I have a view of the old pool of Bethesda. I really should not be writing; my sight is nearly gone.

In case you're interested, you know the Bethesda Pool has all but dried up now. I remember once when it was a thriving spa with hot mineral waters. People came from all over the region just to bathe there. They claimed that it had healing properties — as much mystical as mineral, I fear. I'm enamored with that old pool now because I need its healing waters more than ever. My joints have stiffened with the years, and it seems I live constantly with one ache or pain. Thanks be to God that he counts me worthy to suffer for his cause.

Beecher, I know you know this, but I must remind you that God reserves the right to be God. Mysterious. Awesome. There is none like him. No not one.

Moreover, God makes hard statements. God makes stern demands. God asks hard questions. What makes you think that hard questions will have easy answers? What makes you think that we need to know all the answers? Or that if we knew the answers we would understand what they mean? Abraham discovered that God will do right. Is that enough for you?

You are quite correct, my son, we are not vessels, we are not pots. Whether we are inanimate vessels or animate flesh, he who creates insures that we have structural integrity. It seems unreasonable, this cosmic stress test, but as you might say, he knows how much you can bear!

One word of caution, Beecher. Preaching is not a process of telling the congregation what you think. No one really cares, nor should they, about what you think. The task of proclamation is to faithfully declare what he says through you. We must be faithful to that proclamation even when we do not fully understand or comprehend the word we preach. Others can only point to the light, but he remains and ever shall be the source of light. Only in him is the truth of the Word to be focused and secured. He who speaks in lightning flash and thunder roll is able to unravel the mysteries of his Word. Remember, we see through a glass darkly and when that which is perfect is come (even the sure knowledge of God), then that which is in part shall be done away. Isaiah was correct. His ways are not ours; his thoughts are not our thoughts.

Isn't it strange how God treats those of us who preach his Word so differently? There you sit wondering what to preach and dreading every moment of it. Here I sit praying that on tomorrow I shall still have body and strength to preach and loving every minute of it. How unfair of God! And to think, he did not even ask if we approved of his process!

No, Beecher, we are more than vessels, we are more than pots. God makes use of that which is before him, whether man or metal. It does indeed appear that God is unfair when we are faced with the difficulty of unnecessary human tragedy and suffering and needless privation and starvation among our brothers and sisters. But, I ask you, is God fair when he strives with us still? Is God fair when he retains rather than rejects? Is God fair when he remakes us — over and over and over again? Is it enough to know, as I have heard others say, that he is too good to err and too wise to make a mistake? One thing alone makes sense out of this nonsense. God is not through with the process; he is not through with us! Glory!

> Grace, mercy, and peace,
> Paul

P.S.: By the way, Beecher. I've been beaten with more stripes of the lash than I can count. I've been mobbed, spat upon, ridiculed, and rejected. I am crippled, I walk with a limp, my nose is hooked, my face is red, my eyebrows meet in the middle of my forehead, and I have no family support at all. I wonder what God wants to make out of me? Ah, well! I may be a mess, but I'm his mess!

11

WHAT DOES GOD WANT NOW?

PROLOGUE

Washington, D. C.

Dear Paul:

With the passing of every day it seems that I am becoming more and more like you. For some reason, even though my computer is available, I felt compelled to write to you as you would me—with pen. More importantly, however, with each day I sense a blending of spirits, a harmony of hearts, a merging of souls between us. God be praised for the fellowship we share with each other and in our Lord and Savior Jesus Christ to whom be glory and honor forever and ever.

It is now four o'clock in the morning. I have been awakened from sleep by my desire to write to you, but also by the aches and pains of my body. Yesterday I baptized thirty-seven, Paul, and even though I had help I can still feel the stress and strain. (Paul, did you baptize by immersion? Maybe the Catholics and the Episcopalians are right!) I do not complain, however. These are glorious pains I feel, for they permit me to suffer for the cause of Christ. These pains of mine are testimony to the triumph of the gospel and a sure witness to the foolishness of our preaching. Is this what you meant by "bearing in (your) body the marks of the

Lord Jesus"? I am sure that it is not. How marvelous
it is, however, to be marked by him, for him.

There is so much I need to say to you and time
grows so short. Even now, with the writing of these
words, there is an unexplainable sorrow, a heaviness of
heart, that has consumed my spirit. I know we are
separated by the centuries, but we shall soon walk together on the same shore. Writing is such an insufficient and imprecise tool. How often we hide behind
our words and use our favorite phrases as the shield to
prevent others from knowing who we <u>really</u> are and
what we really think. Soon we shall be absent from the
body, the last enemy shall be destroyed, death will lose
again and we shall be able then to shake glad hands
with the elders and with each other. We shall talk for
an eon and still have more to share. And so shall we
ever be with the Lord.

As I have reviewed our correspondence, Paul, it
seems the more I know the less I know. I know the
large brush strokes of your life, but the fine points of
your personality—the nuances on your life's canvas—
you seem carefully to have preserved. How strange it is
that a public personality is able to remain such a private person.

Please forgive me if this question seems impertinent
or too bold an intrusion on your privacy, but how do
you spend your days, Paul? What consumes your hours?
You have shared so much of the big events in your
life—the Damascus Road, the jailings and beatings, the
courtroom drama, your travels, your writings—but what
are the day-to-day strains on your life?

I raise this question because I am not sure that the
parallels of ministry from the first century are appropriate in the twentieth. The kind of ministry which you
shared was sufficient and significant in the context of
that time, your time. Many of us today are grappling
with the issue of "contextualizing" the ministry and the
preaching event in order that we not be time-locked

into a first-century concept of life and spiritual development which may or may not be relevant to contemporary needs.

Preachers are not preachers any more, Paul. By and large, we are organizers, administrators, strategists, consultants, politicians, economists, social workers, historians, philosophers, counselors, husbands (or wives), parents, urbanologists, community activists, lobbyists, psychiatrists, and necrologists. The list goes on.

Just to give you an idea of my day, Paul, this is what I do. Take last Thursday as a typical example.

8:00—9:00 A.M.   Traffic jam
(Too many people going in the same direction in a hurry to do nothing. They call it "rush hour," but nobody can rush anywhere!)

9:00 A.M.   Read the mail
(I've been trying to do this for three days. There's probably a letter in here from you somewhere.)

9:30 A.M.   Stumble upon a letter from a young woman who wants to commit suicide. I sense this is serious. Spend forty-five minutes in a phone conversation with her and other helping professionals.

10:15 A.M.   Two people are at my door who just must see me.
(I really don't like it when people come without appointments. Ah, well, Jesus had no appointment schedule, so who am I to complain?)

11:15—11:45 A.M.   Return phone calls.
(You don't know what a phone is, do you? The phone is the great scourge of the twentieth century. It is a device that permits people to talk with each other no matter how far away they

may be from each other, whether they want to or not. I could talk with you if you had a phone—all the way from Washington to Tarsus. Wouldn't that be something? My wife says I have a phone growing out of my ear!)

Noon   Funeral—for a non-Christian. We preach to the living and not to the dead. I often wonder what we are expected to do or to say for those who die and who are not "in Christ," as you say.

1:00 P.M.   Lunch—if you can call it that. (My staff thinks I need to lose weight. I eat so much salad I'm developing rabbit ears and there is a serious twitch in my nose.)

1:30 P.M.   Exercise. (Another staff idea. These people are going to kill me in order to get me healthy. But it really helps to clear out the cobwebs. I pretend I'm walking along some dusty road holding a conversation with you and the hour goes by quickly.)

3:00 P.M.   Marriage counseling. Paul, nearly two-thirds of our marriages today end in divorce. I really wish that what you had to say on this issue had been more definitive and, therefore, more helpful.

4:00 P.M.   Telephone conference with the church lawyer and a real estate broker over a little piece of land the church needs to buy. It would help if we had the money to buy it.

5:00 P.M. Staff meeting. I have a staff of twenty-five people, Paul, whose job it is to help me minister to the congregation. (I used to think that having them would make <u>my</u> job easier, but things aren't that simple. The time I save on <u>ministering</u> I now spend on <u>administering</u>. Life is not fair, Paul!)

7:30 P.M. Meet with one of the choirs to discuss a spiritual problem. This one requires real sensitivity. I need to assure them of my love for them, but at the same time provide the spiritual guidance they seem so desperately to need.

8:30 P.M. I'm putting my coat on to go home, but there are three more people at the door. Three quick five-minute conferences. When will I learn to say no?

8:50 P.M. Headed home again. Can hardly keep my eyes open.

9:20 P.M. Arrive at home. (The big news of the day? This is the night I have to take out the trash. Some "hot-shot" preacher I am!)

Nevertheless, I am exhausted. What else can I give? What else does God want? And you have the chutzpah to tell me that God is not satisfied? I must now give my body as a living sacrifice? What does it mean? How do I preach this word? Paul, you make me so angry I could scream! You are so demanding. So unrelenting. So aggravatingly straightforward. And I hear so much of you in my preaching. I am not sure I like it. Write me back and let me know if you do.

Pax,

A burned-out preacher!
Beecher

Sermon: WHAT DOES GOD WANT NOW?
A LIVING SACRIFICE

> I beseech you therefore, brethren, by the mercies of God, that ye present your bodies a living sacrifice, holy, acceptable unto God, which is your reasonable service (Romans 12:1).

I have come today with a word that is at once disturbing, distressing, disruptive, and depressive. This word that is mine to share with you comes, as you know, from the stylus of a preacher in Corinth. This distressing word was placed in a letter that was addressed to "all that be at Rome," but for some strange reason it seems to be a word that is addressed to your name and to my name as well.

I have a word that may cause you to be ill at ease with the practice of religion as you have come to know it.

I have a word that may cause some questions about the focus of your faith and the content of your commitment.

I have a word that may make you squirm on the padded pews of your brand of comfortable Christianity.

I have a word that may stop you in your tracks of pseudo piety, presumptuous religiosity, and self-indulgent spirituality. And so, in all honesty, in all fairness, perhaps you may want to leave by the nearest exit now because I assure you that I have a word that is at once disturbing, distressing, disruptive, and depressive.

Now you may be disturbed to discover that whatever you have been doing as a part of your Christian witness, it may not be enough.

Whatever you have been doing as a testimony to your religious lifestyle, it is inadequate and insufficient.

If today you are tired and worn out and stressed out because the church enterprise requires so much of your time and consumes so much of your energy, and because it saps so much of your creative and intellectual forces with seemingly little in return—whatever it is that has you tired—it is still not enough. There is something else that God wants.

I know you did not want to hear this word, but no matter how much you have given of time and talent and treasure, it is not enough. Whether you've been involved in church work or the work of the church, it is not enough. There is something else that God wants.

You won't mind if I tell you that it is of no consequence how long you have been a part of the church. You may count the years of your membership by decades and by scores, but your count won't count. If you've been coming to the church year after year and week after week and Sunday after Sunday, and if the church door can't creak without your walking in, still I must tell you that it is not enough.

It is not enough. There's something else that God wants.

I regret that I must be the bearer of bad news, but it is required that I tell you that, even if you hold positions of leadership in the church . . .

- Even if you have that coveted position of high visibility within the church,
- Even if you have gained so much on the spiritual weight scale that there are those who listen to your teaching and follow your direction,
- Even if it's a proven fact that you have such high leadership skills that even you believe that the church can't function without you,
- Even if you have come to the point that the value of your leadership is common knowledge in the congregation and, no matter how large the crowd is on Sunday morning, you *know* your seat is always reserved,

It may be disruptive, but I need to tell you it is not enough. There's something else that God wants.

I hope that I remembered to tell you that this word I have today may be disturbing and distressing and disruptive and depressive, because I have the unfortunate assignment of telling you that even though you are a tither—you bring your tithes and offerings to the storehouse . . .

It took you a while, but you finally decided to *give* God what already *belonged* to him.

Even though now you are a tither and you do give that 10

percent and now you're just waiting on the windows of heaven to open up . . .

You are now a tither and you've decided to do God a favor and give him this large sum out of your weekly earnings—but it still is not enough.

I am aware, and painfully so, that this is a difficult word. It is a word that we did not want to hear. Strange as it may seem, I must add to this misery by telling you that even when we gather to worship, whatever we do may not be enough.

- We come here for worship, we sing our songs, the anthem stirs our hearts, the gospel stirs our feet, but it is not enough.
- We are programmed by the same program to pray the same prayers and preach the same sermon and give the same dollar, but it is not enough.
- We wear our uniforms and wear our badges and squeeze in tight on crowded pews, but it is not enough.
- We say "Amen" and lift up holy hands and clap our hands and sometimes we even shout, but when it's all over, it is not enough.

The problem is that typically our worship is designed for us to get what we want, but worship is not authentic worship until God gets what he wants. Whatever we are doing in the religious enterprise, whether our membership or leadership, our tithes or our worship—somewhere in the process God ought to get what he wants. I do not know how it has occurred, but somewhere in the process of the religious enterprise we developed the notion that when we come to worship we ought to get what we want. But God sees to it that you get what you want every day.

- With every breath you take, you get what you want.
- With every step you take, you get what you want.
- When the Lord puts a roof over your head, you get what you want.
- When the Lord puts food on your table, you get what you want.

- When the Lord puts clothes on your back, you get what you want.
- When the Lord puts you in a downtown job and puts money in your bank account, you get what you want!

Even when you think you are deprived, and when you think you are handicapped by some personal or physical or financial deficiency, it is still true that if you are able to say "good morning!" you've already gotten what you want!

But the question I want to raise is: for all of your coming and going in the church and around the church, for all of your sitting in worship in church, I'd like to know, when does God get what God wants?

I hear folk saying, "I went to church today and I didn't get anything out of it."

Have you ever considered that what goes on in church is not for you?

- Worship is not a time to get, it's a time to give.
- Worship is not something that comes for you, it comes from you.

Whenever we gather in this place of worship, it's time for God to get something.

> God gets the glory,
> God gets the praise,
> God gets the honor,
> God is worshiped because God is worthy!

Maybe instead of serving ourselves maybe we ought to concentrate on serving him.

Maybe instead of singing what we want to hear maybe we ought to sing something that he wants to hear.

I am convinced that no matter what we have been doing as a part of our Christian witness it is not enough because there is something else that God wants!

If by chance this word of the insufficiency and inadequacy of the contemporary religious enterprise has in anyway been disturbing or distressing, perhaps you are able to imagine the force and effect which Paul's words had on those who were a part of that first-century church at Rome to which he wrote. Just consider their work and consider their witness.

These were they who framed a faith when the Greeks called it foolishness and the Jews called it a stumbling block.

▪ But to them Paul says, it's not enough.

These were they who joined the church when there was no church; these were they who were converted by uneducated evangelists, who were convicted by illiterate and unlettered fishermen, and who were led to Christ by the preaching of one who admitted that he was the last to see Jesus.

▪ But to them Paul says, it's not enough.

These were they who came to church when the only sign and symbol they had was an old rugged cross that served to remind them of an ignominious death on a blood-soaked hill outside the city walls of Jerusalem on a miserable day that somebody oxymoronically called Good Friday.

▪ But to them Paul says, it is not enough.

These were they who, even when they read Paul's epistle, could only be certain that soon and very soon they would be discovered in their catacomb sanctuary and then be led to their death in Nero's Colosseum.

▪ But to them Paul says, it is not enough.

It is not enough. There's something else that God wants. But tell me: what does God want *now*?

If everything else is to no avail, what does God want now?

If our membership has no substance, and if our leadership has no lasting effect, and if our tithes and our offerings cannot assure our redemption or our salvation, I'd like to know, what does God want now?!

It would be a tragedy to go through all of this work and worship and spend all of this time and give all this money and still not give back what God wants.

What a tragedy to discover after all your years of coming to church and singing in the choir and going to meeting after meeting . . .

After all your attempts at being religious in this life in order to gain a home in the afterlife . . .

What a tragedy after struggling week after week just to get

here to find a seat, after all of this to discover that you still have not given what God wants.

The question is pertinent and important: What does God want now?

Paul says it rather clearly:

> I beseech you therefore, brethren, by the mercies of God, that ye present your bodies a living sacrifice, holy, acceptable unto God.

Now, in the first instance, what God wants are Christians who are more interested in *expressing* than they are in *impressing*. Far too much of what we pass off for religion is designed to impress others about something about ourselves and not to express something about God or how he is working in our lives realistically.

- When you give so that somebody else sees what you put in the plate—that's designed to impress.
- When you carry your Bible just so folk can see you carry your Bible—that's designed to impress.
- When you come to church just so you can be seen—that's designed to impress.

But I'll tell you what—when you present your body *you're not trying to impress*.

- When you cast aside self,
- When you decide to offer your flesh and your bone, your soul and your sinew,
- When you just lay yourself on the altar,
- When you lay yourself prostrate before his throne,
- When you put yourself at his disposal and mean it and make yourself available for his use,

you're not trying to impress.

But Paul says God doesn't need you to impress him. How can you impress God?

After all, you were conceived in sin and shaped in iniquity. How will you impress God?

You were not there when he laid the foundation for the world.

You were not there when he called things that were not and made them into things that are.

How will you impress God?

Even your righteousness is but as filthy rags in his sight.

Paul says, "Present your bodies."

That's an expression of commitment: "Present your bodies."

That's an expression of authentic faith and unquestioning trust: "Present your bodies."

Not because you *want* to, but because you have to: "Present your bodies."

Nobody can make you do it, you must willingly do it: "Present your bodies."

Not because you want the world to see *you*, but because *you* want to see *him*.

That's what God wants. God does not need you to impress. He wants you to express.

Look again to what Paul really says about what God wants:

> I beseech you therefore, brethren,
> by the mercies of God,
> that ye present your bodies
> a living sacrifice.

Perhaps the second thing that God wants is a *living sacrifice*. Now you must understand that the Judaic sacrificial system was based on the concept that God could not be pleased without sacrifice. They brought the doves, they brought the lambs, they brought the goats, but just as soon as they got there, death took the sacrifice. What the Jews had was not a sacrifice that celebrated life but a sacrifice that resulted in death.

But God does not want a dead sacrifice—he wants a living sacrifice. Isaiah understood what God required and wrote it down (1:11): God said, "I've had enough of your burnt offerings of rams and the fat of fed beasts; I do not delight in the blood of bulls or of lambs or of he goats."

God wants something else. God cannot use a dead sacrifice. God wants a living sacrifice. God cannot use anything that is dead. A whole lot of folk are in church, but they're dead.

A whole lot of folk have names on the roll, but they're dead. In the number, but dead.

No zeal, no life, no enthusiasm, not pentecostal fire for the Lord—just dead.

Sitting in a sea of shouting and bathing in an ocean of Holy Ghost, but they sit stiff as a corpse and as cold as a cadaver—dead.

But God wants a living sacrifice.

> A living sacrifice says,
> Use my hands and use my feet.
> A living sacrifice says,
> Here am I, Lord, send me.
> A living sacrifice says
> I'll go where you want me to go!

Black folk have always known what it is to be a living sacrifice.

The society had determined that death would be our destiny, but through the experience we learned to be a "living" sacrifice.

Perhaps your mother didn't have much food, but she knew how to scrimp and save and make do with leftovers, and somehow every day she fixed a meal fit for a king. Love knows how to be a living sacrifice.

Some mothers and fathers never went to schools themselves. They never walked across a stage for diplomas or degrees, but they worked from sunup to sundown so that their children could have the things they never had. That's a living sacrifice.

We are where we are today, the great-grandchildren of slaves, the great-great-grandchildren of those who came to these shores like cattle on slave ships through the middle passage and endured the ships. They endured the chains, they lived through the master's lash. They picked cotton from first light to dusk and dark in order that we could go to school and wear three-piece suits and drive our BMWs. They suffered and bled to bring us, in the words of Jesse Jackson, from "gunny sacks to Cadillacs." That's a living sacrifice.

Let me remind you that there are only two kinds of sacrifice. The first is the sacrifice of reconciliation.

> Long years ago God needed a sacrifice
>   that would atone for man's sin.
> God needed a sacrifice that would reconcile
>   a gracious God with a sin-filled world.
> God needed a sacrifice that would reconcile
>   the creature with the Creator.
> God needed a sacrifice that would make
>   sinful man just before his God.

But man cannot give God the sacrifice of reconciliation. Cain brought his sacrifice to the altar, but God told Cain, "That won't do."

Abraham took Isaac to the altar and laid him there as a sacrifice. But God send word to Abraham, "Isaac won't do."

As a consequence, God sent Jesus.

He would not take Abraham's son. He had to send his own Son.

- God sent Jesus: to wash away your sins and my sins by the shedding of his blood.
- God sent Jesus: to atone at one time for you and for me.
- God sent Jesus: "God was in Christ reconciling the world unto himself."
- God sent Jesus: "God so loved the world that he gave his only begotten Son."

> You cannot save yourself;
> That's why God sent Jesus.
>
> You can't make a way for yourself;
> That's why God sent Jesus.

Man cannot give God the sacrifice of reconciliation.
But listen to what Paul says:

> I beseech you therefore, brethren, by the mercies of God, that ye present your bodies a living sacrifice, holy, acceptable unto God, which is your reasonable service.

Man cannot give God the sacrifice of reconciliation, but once you have been reconciled, once your sins have been forgiven and your transgressions washed away you *can* give the sacrifice of celebration and praise. What God wants now is a life that is willing to praise him for whatever life brings—sorrows or joys, defeats or victories. We must use every opportunity to praise him for his mighty acts. We must use every opportunity to give to him the sacrifice of thanksgiving and praise.

So, praise him with your mind, your heart, and your soul—that's enough!

Praise him with the best resouces of your spiritual being—that's enough!

Praise him with the unselfish giving of your whole self—that's what God wants now, that's an authentic, living sacrifice, that's praise in it's highest and most glorious dimension, and that's enough!

> All to Jesus I surrender,
> All to him I freely give.
> I will ever love and serve him,
> In his presence daily live.
> I surrender All!

INTERLUDE

Washington, D.C.

Dear Paul:

I hope this letter reaches you before you have a chance to respond to my last little offering on "A Living Sacrifice." I decided to send this next one along because it follows so closely on the heels of the other one and because it comes from another look at the same words from your letter. I am always fascinated with the way God's revealed Word shows so many nuances and shades of meaning. How mind-boggling it is to be able to return again and again to the same text and come away with a completely different thought and, as a result, a completely different message.

At any rate, my brother, I have taken the liberty to analyze your words from a different angle and, I hope, properly so. The question I have raised with my hearers and, indeed, the question I raise with you is: What is worship? I assume that the worship of the first century church ... well, what can I assume? We have no clues. Was it formal, informal? Was it warm or cold? Surely there were no printed programs. How did people know when to stand or when to sit? Did you have ushers (persons designated to tell worshipers where to sit) or choirs (groups of persons who blend their voices in the singing of hymns and anthems)? Where did these people come from, anyhow? Did people bring their Bibles and flip through the pages while you preached? If you had no organ (a mechanical instrument that makes the sounds of many horns and pipes and flutes at one time by the hand of one person), who set the tune? More importantly, what songs did you sing? Paul, were you one of those "singing preachers"? Oh, yes, and did you ever have an altar call (asking your worshipers to come forward for a prayer together at the close of the sermon)?

These are really important questions, Paul, because your experience may be normative—we really would like to know what God expects in terms of worship because maybe, after all these years, we're still not doing it right.

By the way, Paul. Do you know what a revival is? Well, from time to time our churches (of the more evangelical kind) have services which extend over a week's time supposedly as a means of evangelizing, of bringing the lost to Christ. These revivals are set in the context of worship, but I wonder sometimes if they really gain the end that we seek. I confess, I've been called all over this country to preach revival after revival, and after all these years I come away wondering how many souls have really been saved, how many lives have really been changed. Are churches really positively affected by them, or are they no more than annual preaching shows where the visiting preacher is able to trot out his or her latest preaching goods? In a word, Paul, I really wonder sometime if the Lord is going to hold us preachers accountable for what may have degenerated into ecclesiastical sideshows which have absolutely nothing to do with winning the world for Christ.

But the question remains: What is worship?

Take a moment then to read both these sermons. I really got caught up in this passage. I think it's my favorite in the whole letter to the Romans because I think it really expresses your complete thought in one sentence.

Pray for me, Paul. It's a struggle to preach. It's a struggle to be what God wants me to be. I am often not sure that I am the sacrifice he wants or that my worship is the worship he desires.

Grace to you, Paul.

Seeking to serve,
Beecher

Sermon: WHAT DOES GOD WANT NOW? REASONABLE WORSHIP

> I beseech you therefore, brethren, by the mercies of God that ye present your bodies a living sacrifice, holy, acceptable unto God, which is your reasonable service (Romans 12:1).

To the casual observer the opening lines of the twelfth chapter of the book of Romans may seem to be no more than a thematic shift or perhaps an insignificant change of mood and emphasis on the part of the aging apostle by whose hand these words were written. However, to those who share with Paul this preaching profession there is no doubt that Paul, the preacher, is now approaching the climax of his sermon. I make this assessment primarily because anyone who has become sensitive over time to the soul and the spirit of this Tarsus-born preacher is aware that we are no longer hearing the words of a theologian. His voice is in crescendo now. No doubt his head is tilted and there is a new urgency to his words which once were marked by formality and precision. Paul is no longer an academician arguing with Jews and Greeks. Paul is now a preacher, and he is arguing for men's souls.

The careful student of Paul's epistle to the Roman church will observe that there has been rapid movement from those opening lines in which Paul sought to define who he was in relation to who they were.

The careful student, with a spiritual ear, has clearly heard Paul as he has spoken of sin and salvation, iniquity and pardon.

The careful student has surely learned as Paul has run the gamut from Judaic legalism and formalism to a new platform of uncompromising trust and liberating faith.

The careful student has seen a rather insecure and vulnerable Paul open up the very innards of his heart and declare that what he really wants, what his heart really desires "for Israel is that she might be saved."

Ultimately, the careful student has soared with Paul as he has come to that climactic assurance that nothing "shall be able to separate us from the love of God, which is in Christ Jesus our Lord."

Now, however, after Paul has spent his time dealing with the weighty matters of justification and sanctification, after Paul has gone to great lengths to define the "wages of sin" and the gift of grace, now Paul puts on his preaching garments and has the temerity and the audacity to suggest that whatever we are doing in the name of religion is not enough.

I didn't say it—Paul said it.

- Paul said that whatever you're doing and you call it religion—it's not enough!
- Whatever you're doing and you call it service—it's not enough!
- However you're spending your time in the work of the church—it's not enough.

▪ And even if you thought that you were doing more than anybody else, Paul told me to tell you—it's not enough.

A question must be raised if Paul is about to come to the close of his writing, and if everything we have done and are doing is not enough, if Paul is not satisfied and God is not impressed, I want to ask: *What does God want now?*

It is, then, in response to this question, "What does God want now?" that Paul answers by saying:

> I beseech you therefore, brethren,
> by the mercies of God,
> that ye present your bodies a living sacrifice,
> holy, acceptable unto God,
> which is your reasonable service.

In the first instance the obvious implication of this text is that

WHAT GOD WANTS NOW IS NOT PART OF US; HE WANTS ALL OF US.

The text says it quite plainly, God does not want a dead sacrifice, God wants a living sacrifice, and it must be "holy and acceptable."

However, Paul suggests that that is not *all* God wants. What God wants, in the second instance, is not simply a living sacrifice but that sacrifice must be part and parcel of what Paul calls "your reasonable service." The word *service* is, in the Greek, the word *latreia* which is defined by the words *ministry,* or *service* or *worship.* So then a varied translation is that God wants us to present our bodies, a living sacrifice, holy and acceptable unto God which is our reasonable *worship.*

That notion of reasonable worship has intrigued me. It has intrigued me, I suppose, primarily because it would not have been necessary for Paul to point out the necessity for reasonable worship were it not for the fact that something was wrong or inappropriate or *unreasonable* in the worship experience of that first-century church. Evidently something was wrong with the worship. Evidently there had come about an improper definition and, as a result, an improper practice of this thing called worship.

Worship was a part of Israel's experience. Was it not David who declared, "O come, let us worship and bow down: let us kneel before the Lord our maker."

Worship was the source of Israel's joy. That same David was heard to exclaim, "I was glad when they said unto me, Let us go into the house of the Lord."

But Paul suggests that what God wants is not just worship for the sake of worship; what God really requires, and what God really wants now, is *reasonable worship.*

It does not take long to discover that this word *reasonable* is derived from the Greek word *logikos* which is the root of our word *logical.* So then, Paul is really saying that God requires logical worship. God requires worship that is the result of rational activity. God requires worship that is the product of a reasoning, functioning mind, or as J. B. Phillips has translated this word, God requires a worship "that is worthy of thinking beings."

Authentic worship must be intelligent worship.

- Participation in church activity is not enough.
- Erecting a building to house the church is not enough.
- Laying down wall-to-wall carpet and putting choirs in robes is not enough.
- Stained-glass windows and chandeliers and pipe organs are not enough.

God is not concerned about where you are, but he is concerned about what you are to become and what your relationship is to be with him. Since he is the author of intelligence, since he is omniscient, omnipotent, and omnipresent, God does not want anything that is haphazard; God doesn't want anything that is less than the best. God wants logical, rational, intelligent, reasonable worship.

The more we examine this word, the more it becomes apparent that maybe we ought to spend some quality time in search of a workable definition for *reasonable worship.* This matter of worship, as you know, has been a matter of some importance since the church began.

You do recall that Jesus held a conversation one day with a

Samaritan woman at the well, and what they talked about, among other things, was this matter of worship.

I seem to recall that that woman was concerned about the *where* of worship, but Jesus was concerned about the *quality* of worship.

That woman was concerned about the *place* of worship, but Jesus was concerned about the *purpose* of worship.

Jesus said to her:

> Woman, . . . the hour cometh when ye shall
> neither in this mountain, nor yet at Jerusalem
> worship the Father. . . .
> But the hour cometh, and now is,
> when the true worshippers shall worship the Father
> in spirit and in truth. . . .
> God is a Spirit:
> and they that worship him
> *must* worship him in spirit and in truth!
>
> (John 4:21–24)

Every time I hear that word from Jesus it convicts me of the fact that all worship is not *true* worship. By force of logic, if there is *true* worship there must also be *false* worship. The ultimate question of worship is the spirit by which we come; the question of importance is whether our worship reveals that which is truth or exalts that which is false. God requires reasonable worship which must be measured by its spirit and its truth.

Toward a Definition of Worship

There is value in determining at the outset what authentic worship is *not*.

First of all, worship is not to be found in the order of worship. The worshiper is often unaware of this, but genuine worship is not to be found in the printed program. Make no mistake about it, the order of worship is there to provide that things be done "decently and in order," but that is not worship. The worship ought to be ordered and orderly.

The organ prelude says: "Be still and know that I am God."

The call to worship is what Howard Thurman calls the "centering moment" that says, "The Lord is in his holy temple; let all the earth keep silence before him."

The reading of Scripture reminds us that the grass will wither and the flower will fade, but the Word of God will stand forever.

The anthem is designed to take a soul that is caught in the muck and mire of life and lift it to a spiritual high where it can soar on melodies fit for the Eternal.

The offering is a time for cheerful givers to "give as it has been given," good measure, pressed down and running over; it is the time to bring the tithes and offerings not because we need to bribe God into something that he will do but because we need to thank God for what he has already done.

The time of preaching is required because Paul says that "it pleased God by the foolishness of preaching to save them that believe."

The claiming of souls is essential because heaven rejoices when just one soul comes home.

The benediction is necessary because you wouldn't want to stay all this time and then miss out on the final blessing.

Finally, the organ postlude is not just an unnecessary addendum to the program. It's just the instrument's way of saying that when you leave the worship in the sanctuary, it's time to go to work in the world.

Yet, even if you have all of these elements of worship, you still may not be engaged in *reasonable worship*.

Authentic worship is not in the order of worship. We must be careful with these worship programs. I've been in churches all over the country, and I've never seen any place on the program for the Spirit. We run the danger, with these fancy programs of ours, of de-programming the Holy Ghost.

Authentic worship is not an isolated experience. We live in an age which has nearly lost a generation because of the notion that you could be a Christian and not go to church. There are those who have grown up with the misguided notion that they can have their own church right where they are and, as a consequence, church attendance is unnecessary. How tragic it must be to be satisfied with a religion predicated on isolation. An isolated Christian is a contradiction in terms. It's not just that Hebrews 10:25 says, "Forsake not the assembling of yourselves together." The Bible says that we cannot be isolated from one another because we need one another. Over and over, the Scriptures affirm the mutuality of our need for *one another*.

- Wash one another's feet.
- Prefer one another.
- Be of the same mind toward one another.
- Edify one another.
- Receive one another.
- Admonish one another.
- Care for one another.
- Minister gifts to one another.
- Greet one another.
- Serve one another.
- Bear one another's burdens.
- Forgive one another.
- Comfort one another.
- Exhort one another.
- Fellowship with one another.
- Give hospitality to one another.
- Love one another.
- Pray for one another.

None of these assignments can be achieved alone. We need one another. I insist that authentic worship is not an isolated experience.

Authentic worship is not entertainment. It may well be that the great tragedy of the twentieth-century church may not come as a consequence of what Satan did from the outside but from what we have done in the name of worship from the inside.

Whenever worship is more concerned about exciting content than it is about serious intent—that's entertainment.

When worship centers on who's singing and not on who's saved—that's entertainment.

When worship has degenerated into a weekly fashion parade—that's entertainment.

Whenever the aides to the worship become the object of worship—that's entertainment.

Whenever people are more concerned about which preacher is preaching than they are about what the preacher has to say—that's entertainment.

Whenever the offering is taken up to satisfy the needs of those on the inside and not a word is said about the need for ministry to those on the outside—that offering is just another way of paying for entertainment.

Authentic worship is not in the order of worship, authentic worship is not an isolated experience, and authentic worship is not entertainment. Paul says, if that's what you're involved in, it's not enough because what God requires is "reasonable worship."

We have examined what reasonable worship is *not*. To be intellectually responsible we must also examine what reasonable worship *is* or should be. Warren W. Wiersbe, in his book entitled *Real Worship*, suggests that worship occurs whenever we congregate, celebrate, commemorate, communicate, or contemplate. But I'm not satisfied that this really helps you know what Paul means by the phrase *reasonable worship*.

On the other hand, if I might suggest a definition or two I might be inclined to tell you that *reasonable worship is often unreasonable worship*. Sometimes because of life's circumstances worship becomes unreasonable.

Don't you find it so?

- It's hard to worship when you are battered and bruised.
- It's hard to worship when your ship comes in and there's nothing on it for you.
- It's hard to worship when you've given your best and still it looks like the Lord has forgotten all about you.
- It's hard to worship when the burden is almost more than you can bear, and each day bitter tears become your cup.
- It's hard to worship when it looks as if God is just not fair.

Perhaps that was the predicament in which Abraham stood. Here God had waited until the sunset years of his life to give him a son. Isaac was Sarah's joy and Abraham's dream.

Then God says "Abraham, give him up." That's unreasonable.

"Abraham, you can't have him any longer." That's unreasonable.

"Abraham . . . take now thy son, thine only son Isaac . . . and offer him . . . for . . . an offering." That's unreasonable.

But then, the Book says, Abraham "lifted up his eyes, and saw the place afar off," and Abraham told those who were traveling with him, "Abide here . . . and I and the lad will go yonder and worship."

Abraham is on his way to the sacrifice, but Abraham says, "I'm on my way to worship." That's unreasonable.

Abraham had his son in one hand and a knife to slit his throat in the other, and yet Abraham says, "I'm on my way to worship." That's unreasonable.

Abraham is one step from seeing everything he had hoped and dreamed for taken away, and yet Abraham says, "I'm on my way to worship." That's unreasonable.

By way of analysis, the reason Abraham was able to worship was that he knew that God was able to handle the *unreasonableness of life.*"

Very often worship is not worship until you don't understand why you worship, but you worship anyhow.

Worship is not worship until you're able to lean and depend on him whom you worship!

- When you can't understand, worship him!
- When you can't see your way, worship him!
- When what he asks is more than you have to give, worship him!
- When you must surrender that for which you would give life itself, worship him!

Worship is not worship until reasonable worship is unreasonable.

In the last analysis *reasonable worship, or the worship with which God is pleased, may be likened to the worship of the prophet Isaiah.*

You do remember Isaiah? It was Isaiah who went to great lengths to describe his experience of reasonable worship. Isaiah said it was: "In the year the King Uzziah died I saw also the Lord sitting upon the throne."

Did you hear what Isaiah said? He said, *"I saw also the Lord."* Whenever you have reasonable worship it enables you to see the Lord. You might not see who's sitting next to you, but you will see the Lord. You might not see the preacher, but you will see the Lord.

What else happened, Isaiah?

"Above [the temple] stood the seraphim: each one had six wings; with twain he covered his face, and with twain he covered his feet and with twain he did fly. And one cried unto another and said, Holy, Holy, Holy, is the Lord of hosts."

In other words, not only did Isaiah see something, he also *heard something.* In reasonable worship you ought to hear something. Paul insists that "faith comes by hearing, and hearing by the word of God."

When you have an experience of reasonable worship you ought to go away saying, "He speaks and the sound of his voice is so sweet the birds hush their singing."

When you have a reasonable worship you ought to go away from that encounter saying: "I heard the voice of Jesus say come unto me and rest, lay down thou weary one, lay down, thy head upon my breast."

What else happened, Isaiah?

"The posts of the door moved at the voice of him that cried . . ."

Not only did Isaiah see something, and not only did Isaiah hear something, but Isaiah felt something. It's not a reasonable worship if you don't feel something. I declare we've got enough comatose Christians and enough anesthetized church members. If you have an experience of intelligent, rational, reasonable worship, you just ought to feel something. I wouldn't come Sunday after Sunday and not feel something. Ultimately, faith and feeling are not antithetical, they are complimentary.

What else happened, Isaiah? I know you saw something. I know you heard something. I know you felt some things, but what else happened in this reasonable worship?

"I heard the voice of the Lord, saying, Whom shall I send, and who will go for us? Then said I, here am I; send me."

Worship is not reasonable worship until you do something. Worship is not worship until you volunteer for service in the army of the King. Worship is not worship until you put your hand to the plow and never look back. Worship is not worship until you can say, "For Christ I'll live, and for Christ I'll die."

Worship is not worship until you can say:

- "If the Lord needs somebody, here am I, send me!"

Twenty-eight years ago I stood to preach my trial sermon. Twenty-four years ago I knelt for ordination to the gospel ministry.

I said it then, and I'll say it now:

- "If the Lord needs somebody, send me!"

EPILOGUE

Rome

H. Beecher Hicks, Jr.
Metropolitan Baptist Church
Washington, D. C. 20009

Dear Reverend Hicks:

Although you may not know me, I feel as though I have known you for some time now. My name is Barnabas, Paul's traveling companion for many years. Paul has spoken of you and shared your writings and your sermons with me.
Unfortunately, most of your material was lost in a shipwreck somewhere near the island of Melita. Maybe you have already heard the news of the storm last winter. It was a violent storm. I don't believe that anyone on board ship was prepared for what they experienced that night. There was much loss of life, and many only made it to shore hanging on to the splintered

*leftovers of the ship. Through it all, however — storm, rain,
shipwreck — they finally made port at Paul's long-sought Rome.*

*I am writing because Paul would have wanted me to. Paul
gave his life for the Christ he loved today. He would have
wanted you to know. For those of us who watched, it was
gruesome. For those of us who knew Paul's faith, it was
glorious. No. For Paul, his death was his gain.*

*I have seen many people die here in Rome. They are "babes
in Christ," and when death comes near I have seen the silent
fear written in their eyes and chiseled in their brows. They do
not speak, these new Christian converts, for they fear two
deaths — the death of life with Nero, the death of a life that
must be lived without Christ. I am not sure that many
understand fully why they have chosen to die; but I can tell
that despite their hesitancy, they sense they have chosen a better
life.*

*But Paul? Paul was a new experience for the Christians at
Rome. Over six decades had taken their toll on his body. He
was not the strident bold Paul we had first seen in Damascus
or the fiery energetic preacher we had followed as he made his
journeys to the churches in Asia Minor. We saw something else
today. Maturity. Confidence. Assurance. A holy immunity from
fear.*

*His speech before Nero was brief — but eloquent. His
mastery of words was never sharper. The whole Roman court
stood mute as Paul argued the case for Christ. We knew his
conversion was real. We felt the crucifixion. We died as Christ
died. We rose with him on resurrection morning. If ever a man
believed as he preached and preached as he believed, it was Paul.
How proud I was to know him and to have served with him. I
shall be prouder still to die as he did, for I know that my days
are few.*

*The Colosseum was filled. Christians and lions. The bodies,
the blood. But for Paul, it would not be lions — a chopping
block. His body was bent with years of beatings and lashings.*

Age had not been kind to Paul. But today Paul walked more erectly than I had ever seen, his head thrown back. He no longer walked with that crippling limp. There was even a gleam of triumph in his eyes. Would you believe it, he actually looked as though he wanted to die, as though he wanted to be sacrificed to the slaughter. But he was not sacrificed; he volunteered to suffer, to bleed, and to die for the Christ of God.

They sensed it. Every spectator of Rome knew that there was something different about this man whose head would soon roll in the sawdust of Nero's bloody playground. But when Paul stood there, the sun blazing with the firey darts of heaven, all one could hear was the sound of silence. No one spoke but Paul.

I have fought the good fight.
I have kept the faith.
I have finished my course!

Only three sentences. The greatest sermon I ever heard Paul preach.

And then God took him.

How long shall we preach before you and I are privileged to live and die like Paul?

Deacon Epaphroditus greets you in the name of Christ, and all the saints salute you. Keep your sermon notes handy, Beecher. Soon — very soon — you and Paul will be able to continue. Correspondence is over — next time, conversation.

Grace be with you now and ever,
Barnabas

12

FROM THEOLOGY TO DOXOLOGY

Sermon: FROM THEOLOGY TO DOXOLOGY

Now to him that is of power to stablish you according to my gospel, and the preaching of Jesus Christ, according to the revelation of the mystery, which was kept secret since the world began, But now is made manifest, and by the scriptures of the prophets, according to the commandment of the everlasting God, made known to all nations for the obedience of faith: To God only wise, be glory through Jesus Christ for ever. Amen (Romans 16:25–27).

In the main, the book of Romans is a spiritual odyssey, penned by the hand of the apostle Paul, which spans the gamut from theology to doxology. You are aware, of course, that the book of Romans is the clearest and the most concise statement of Christian doctrine and belief. This preacher from Tarsus, once Saul now Paul, did not merely participate in the founding of churches, but his was the mind that molded its thought, his the hands that wrote the epistles of Christian ecclesiastical concept, his the voice that gave meat and meaning to the Christian understanding of life here as well as life hereafter.

As a consequence, the writing of this epistle to the church at Rome became the philosophical and theological underpinning for a church yet in the embryonic stages of development. From the days of his sojourn with the Christians at Corinth, and with a view of making a journey to be with those to whom he writes, Paul sets his course to speak of what God has done, but in the end he speaks of what God is doing. Paul begins his work as a scholar with something significant to say, and yet he ends his work as a sinner who knows what it is to be saved and as a reject who knows what it is to be redeemed.

Romans, at its beginning, is a Christian apologetic designed for the legalistic Jew and destined for the intellectual Greek. But at its ending, Romans is a Christian affirmation of what God has done through Jesus, not just for the Jew, and not just for the Greek, but for *every one* that believeth. What begins at the cross is for Paul a statment of theology. Yet, as it closes with a word of praise and glory, it becomes a statment of doxology. The book of Romans is a spiritual odyssey, penned by the hand of the apostle Paul, which spans the gamut from theology to doxology.

As we come to Paul's closing words, the careful scholar will want to revisit some of the great high points of Pauline thought. He who examines the essence of Pauline thought will discover that when Paul picks up his pen, he is a thoughtful theologian, but when Paul puts his pen down, he has discovered something to shout about.

Since Romans is a book of the mental as well as the spiritual, and since Romans is reflective of both soul and sense, and since Romans seeks to deal with those issues of both head and heart, for one last time I'd like to take a look at what Paul the theologian has to say and then take a look at what Paul the preacher has to offer.

By way of analysis, I'd like to see what it is that moves Paul from the abyss of sin to the ecstasy of salvation.

I'd like to discover what it is in the offerings of this apostle that is able to take men from rejection to redemption.

I'd like to know, according to Pauline thought, the ground upon which one can stand that will take one from the *hopeless* to the *hopeful*.

Since I must work out my own theology, since as Paul suggests I must "work out my own soul salvation," since I must come to understand how God acts in my own spiritual life, and since I must understand how God acts to take me from what I used to be to what he wants me to be—how God is able to transfer and translate me from my "was-ness" to my "isness" to my "will-be-ness"—I want to find out just how Paul does move from theology to doxology.

The first tenet of Paul's theology is that there is power in the preaching of the gospel. You must be aware that the apostle Paul did not live in an era of preaching prominence. By and large, Judaism was a religion of ceremony. Judaism, in its expressions of worship, was a religion of rite and ritual. And even though prophets prophesied and even though prophets claimed and proclaimed, Israel did not specialize in, Israel had no interest in, Israel made no investment in preaching. But if Paul says anything at all, he says that there is something about the power of preaching.

By the power of preaching, John the Baptist stood one day in the wilderness of Judea and preached one sermon: "Repent, for the kingdom of God is at hand!"

By the power of preaching, Jesus himself stood in the synagogue at Capernaum and cried out: "The spirit of the Lord is upon me for he hath anointed me to preach the gospel to the poor."

By the power of preaching, Jesus could speak and dead men would live. By the power of preaching, Jesus could speak and five thousand men would sit down to be fed. By the power of preaching, even a law-bound, pharasaic, ultra-conservative, rabbinical religionist like Nicodemus would come knocking by night just to hear Jesus say: "Nicodemus, you must be born again."

By the power of preaching, even impetuous, impious, unpredictable Peter could stand to declare God's holy Word and three thousands souls be saved.

Consequently, when Paul began his theological treatise for the church at Rome, he began by saying there is power is preaching. Paul was convinced that:

- Preaching will save.
- Preaching will convert.
- Preaching will redeem.
- Preaching will reclaim lost sheep.
- Preaching will make fractured men whole.

▪ And, in point of fact, preaching will make dead men live again!

A theology of preaching was critically important to the corpus of Pauline thought. In fact, so important was preaching to Paul's ministry that he complained to the Corinthian church: "Woe be unto me if I preach not the gospel." Additionally, Paul spoke of his preaching conviction with these words:

> For I am not ashamed of the gospel of Christ:
> for it is the power of God unto salvation
> to everyone that believeth;
> to the Jew first, and also to the Greek.
>
> (Romans 1:16)

But that's only the first step that leads you from theology to doxology.

In the second instance, Paul's theology not only dealt with the matter of proclamation, but it dealt with the fundamental issue of what faith is and what faith is not. You do recall that the Jews believed that they could live in harmony with God as a result of their strict observance of Judaic law. Paul was convinced, however, that the law had no power to save.

Moreover, Jews believed that they could find the very essence of the spiritual life as a result of their adherence to strict ceremonial and sacrifical laws. But Paul said an animal and blood sacrifice is insufficient. They believed, as well, that somehow their works were all that was necessary to gain entrance into the kingdom. Again Paul objected. Paul's postion was clear:

THE JUST SHALL LIVE BY FAITH!

And what of our sacrifices? What of our tithes and offerings? No matter what the sacrifice—even tithes and offerings—if our heart is not right, if our spirit is not right, if our motive is not pure, the whole process will cast a questioning light on the integrity of our gift. The question is not how much we give, but why. The issue is not the substance of our cash, but the foundation of our faith.

Paul is clear in his argument and in his theological position.

One is not saved by the law. One is not saved by sacrifice. And Paul's ultimate position of interest to his hearers is that even works have no salvific power. What this means for us is that no matter how much work we do in the church and around the church, God won't be pleased if it's all work and no witness. God won't be pleased if it's all just an "outside show." God won't be pleased if your work is done just in order to be seen by men. And that's why it is so critical to understand the meaning of Paul's theme: "The just shall live by faith."

Every day we live is an adventure in faith.

We live by faith—in spite of what we have or what we do not have.

The just live by faith.

We live by faith—even when our pockets are empty and there is no prospect of any change of circumstance.

The just live by faith.

We live by faith—in spite of the fact that we have too many questions and not enough answers.

The just live by faith.

Paul's meaning is clear:

- Faith will help you to hold on a little while longer.
- Faith will lift you when your head is bowed beneath your knees.
- Faith will shield you when enemies gather round.
- Faith will protect you from unseen danger and unknown harm.
- Faith will be the very essence of life itself.

But that's not the only reason that Paul is able to move from a posture of theology to a posture of doxology. Paul is beginning now to move toward doxology when he suggests that not only do we live by faith, but the source of our faith is to be found in the fact that *"God commended his love toward us, in that, while we were yet sinners, Christ died for us."*

No matter what our theological position may be, the reality is that we cannot get from theology to doxology until we go by the cross. You see . . .

The thing that takes me from the shame of my sin to the

assurance of my salvation is that somewhere along the line I get to go to the cross.

The one event of history that takes me from the tyranny of the law to the liberating influence of God's love is that somebody told me that down around the cross there is a fountain filled with blood.

The one circumstance that intersects and intertwines divine and human history is simply that one Friday afternoon Jesus died to save my soul.

The essence of the gospel according to Paul and the thought that takes Paul along on his journey from theology to doxology is that Jesus did not die when we got right, he died while we were still wrong.

Jesus did not die after all our sins were forgiven and all our sins were washed away.

- He died while we were still dirty.
- He died while we were still undeserving.
- He died while it didn't make sense to die.
- He died while the world didn't understand why he was dying.

I must add, as I take my leave, a footnote to this sermonic offering on Paul's systematic theology as a means of justifying what it is that brings Paul from theology to doxology.

Paul, the Jew, is able to look back across the God-directed history of Israel as a people. Paul, the man, is able to look back across the rough hills and the dangerous valleys of his own spiritual growth and development. Paul, the preacher, is able to look back on what he was and what he has become. Paul, the preacher, is able to make an honest assessment of his own sins and shortcomings. Paul, the preacher, is able to come to a rather painful and poignant self-analysis and then, with bold honesty, he is able to write down in his own psychiatric journal that he is, in fact, a "wretched man," always able to do evil but never able to do good.

But when it's all said and done—when Paul has made his final analysis of his weakness and his strength, when Paul looks clearly at his wickedness and his wantoness, when Paul surveys how far the Lord has brought him from that blinding, direction-changing, Damascus-Road experience until now when he is able to see the new creature he has become—it is only after this painful and torturous analysis that Paul comes to declare:

> And we know that all things
> work together for good to them that love God,
> to them who are the called according to his purpose!

That's what does it. That's what brings me from my theology to my doxology. That's what enables me to say:

No matter how hard it has been, all things . . .

No matter how threatening the storm clouds have been, all things . . .

No matter how lonely and friendless I have been, all things . . .

No matter how saturated by sin or traduced by transgressions, all things . . .

No matter how painful my past, all things work together for good!

All things work together?

I don't know how they work together.

I just know that somehow God is working it out.

- Whatever the problem, God is working it out.
- Whatever the perplexity, God is working it out.
- Whatever the roadblock or the stumbling stone, God is working it out.

He's got the whole world in his hands, and that means that God is working it out.

And so, the good news is: *All things* work together for good for them that love the Lord.

Paul now comes to the end of his theology. We suggested, at the outset, that the book of Romans is a spiritual odyssey, penned by the hand of the apostle Paul, which spans the gamut from theology to doxology. Here in the sixteenth chapter, with this postscript, as it were, tacked on to the body of his epistle,

Paul has now come to the completion of his work. Paul's theology is clear:

- Man is a sinner, but God is just.
- Man cannot justify himself, yet God, through Jesus, not only declares man justified, but he makes man just.
- Man is guilty, but God will not condemn. Indeed, God reviews the charges, erases the sentence, pays the fine, and pronounces "Case dismissed."
- Sin abounds, but grace much more abounds.
- The gospel must be preached.

The just shall live by faith.

While we were yet sinners Christ died for us.

All things work together for good.

Taken on the whole, this is the sum and substance of Paul's theology.

However, now that the work is complete, now that the Word has been declared, now that we have the theological frame of reference, Paul, at the closing of his epistle, writes that there is one other thing that we ought to do:

"Receive Phoebe, greet Priscilla and Aquila, salute Epanetus, greet Mary, salute Andronicus and Junia, greet Amplias" . . . and the list goes on.

That tells us that we must not forget each other. Just because we have the theological frame of reference, doesn't mean we can forget each other.

Salute one another with a holy kiss.

Don't take one another for granted.

What sense does it make to have all this religion and not love one another?

What sense does it make to go to our churches and make all our "ecclesiastical noise" and not care for one another? Christians live in community. Don't forget one another.

Finally Paul comes to the end of his epistle when he declares: "Now to him!" (16:25).

- Now to him: The God of our weary years . . .
- Now unto him: The God of our silent tears . . .

- Now unto him: The God of Abraham, Isaac, and Jacob . . .
- Now unto him: The God of Harriet Tubman and Booker T. and Emmet Till . . .
- Now unto him: The God of Medgar, Malcolm, and Martin . . .
- Now unto him: Our way maker and our company keeper . . .
- Now unto him: Our walking cane and our leaning post . . .

What about that God, Paul?

"To God only wise, be glory." That's the word: glory! That's doxology: glory! You see, when you start talking about God you're talking about praise. And if you look back into the word *glory*, it is the sum and substance of what we call doxology.

Glory is the word of recital at the end of every hymn. *Glory* is the word that comes at the end of every benediction and the end of every prayer. At every high moment somebody ought to say "Glory!"

Our religion is not complete with theology alone. We need theology, but we must also have doxology.

- *Theology* is mind power, but *doxology* is soul power.
- *Theology* asks "why," but *doxology* says "thank you!"
- *Theology* is concerned about God's omniscience, but *doxology* affirms God's omnipotence.
- *Theology* is sometimes nothing more than debate and dialogue, but *doxology* is a hymn that takes you from hardship to hallelujah!
- *Theology* is something to think about, but *doxology* is something to shout about.

Make no mistake about it, our theology is important. However, at life's ultimate level, philosophical theology can only take you so far. You can understand the theology of Barth or Bultmann, Tillich or Bonhoeffer, Niebuhr or Brunner. You can understand the religious philosophy of Kant or Hegel or the social gospel of Rauschenbush. You can be a systematic theologian or a practical theologian or a liberation theologian. You may have the finest interpretive skills. You may have the latest data of biblical research. You may be a skilled exegete or a renowned homiletician and you may exercise the greatest hermeneutical skill in dividing the word of truth. But unless God gets the glory, unless God gets the praise, unless your theology brings you to doxology, it will have no effect. All authentic theology must ultimately bring us to the doxology of praise:

> Praise God from whom all blessings flow,
> Praise Him all creatures here below,
> Praise Him above ye heavenly hosts,
> Praise Father, son, and Holy Ghost!